From the Millpond to the Sea

From the Millpond to the Sea
One River, Three Tributaries, Four Dams

AKIKO BUSCH

excelsior editions
State University of New York Press
Albany, New York

Cover Credit: Anne Diggory, *Jammed*, 1993, oil on canvas, 14½ × 27 in.

Published by State University of New York Press, Albany

© 2025 Akiko Busch

All rights reserved

Printed in the United States of America

No part of this book may be used or reproduced in any manner whatsoever without written permission. No part of this book may be stored in a retrieval system or transmitted in any form or by any means including electronic, electrostatic, magnetic tape, mechanical, photocopying, recording, or otherwise without the prior permission in writing of the publisher.

Links to third-party websites are provided as a convenience and for informational purposes only. They do not constitute an endorsement or an approval of any of the products, services, or opinions of the organization, companies, or individuals. SUNY Press bears no responsibility for the accuracy, legality, or content of a URL, the external website, or for that of subsequent websites.

EU GPSR Authorised Representative:
Logos Europe, 9 rue Nicolas Poussin, 17000, La Rochelle, France
contact@logoseurope.eu

Excelsior Editions is an imprint of State University of New York Press

For information, contact State University of New York Press, Albany, NY
www.sunypress.edu

Library of Congress Cataloging-in-Publication Data

Name: Busch, Akiko author.
Title: From the Millpond to the sea : one river, three tributaries, four
    dams / Akiko Busch.
Description: Albany : State University of New York Press, [2025]. | Series:
    Excelsior editions | Includes bibliographical references and index.
Identifiers: LCCN 2025011079 | ISBN 9798855804287 (pbk. : alk. paper) |
    ISBN 9798855804294 (ebook)
Subjects: LCSH: Dams—Environmental aspects—Hudson River Valley (N.Y.
    and N.J.) | Dam retirement—Hudson River Valley (N.Y. and N.J.) |
    Biodiversity—Hudson River Valley (N.Y. and N.J.) | Hudson River Valley
    (N.Y. and N.J.)—Environmental conditions—21st century | Hudson River
    (N.Y. and N.J.)—Environmental conditions—21st century
Classification: LCC GE155.H83 B87 2025 | DDC 363.7/05097473—dc23/eng/20250721
LC record available at https://lccn.loc.gov/2025011079

For the stewards of the Hudson River and its tributaries

No national frontier that I can think of separates two worlds more dissimilar than the reservoir and the river.

—John McPhee

Sooner or later, the fish will win.

—John Lipscomb

Contents

Preface	ix
From the Millpond to the Stream	1
The Impoundment Preserved: Furnace Pond Dam	29
After the Breach: McKinney Dam	57
The Creek Restored: Shapp Pond Dam	85
Beauty Reconsidered: Jamawissa Creek	109
Streams Reconnected	135
Notes	151
Acknowledgments	157
Selected Bibliography	159
Index	161

Preface

In the spring of 2020, I began working on a project to review our town's geography. The Natural Resources Inventory is a compilation of environmental facts of a given area, in this case the geology and soil, wildlife habitats, land cover, plant species, aquifers, and floodplains of a small area of New York's Hudson Valley. Soon after, the country faced a global pandemic and went into the isolation enforced by Covid-19. I knew that forested areas, geologic formations, soil content, and species habitat were all important, but it was the connectedness of waterways that engaged me most. Later I wondered if it was the word *lockdown* itself that made me especially attentive to the free-flowing paths of rivers and streams. Working with ecologists from the New York State Department of Environmental Conservation (NYSDEC) and the Cornell Cooperative Extension who had created a template with which to assess resources, I became better acquainted with the watershed: its headwater streams, broader creeks, natural trout brooks, basin grades, ponds, and wetlands. Downloading the GIS maps, I found that the geographic information systems I was most drawn to were those of the tributaries I thought I knew so well—where they began, how they met and merged with one another, where they flowed into the Hudson River. All of this was mesmerizing.

Yet at the same time I was tracing these threads and patches in their various shades of blue and green with a cursor across the screen of my laptop, I came to realize how fragmented they had become in the landscape itself. Their incessant flow on the maps I was looking at was a fiction. Whether marginally intact, decaying, or entirely breached, dams had been segmenting these streams and rivers for decades, often for centuries. They once helped to power mills for grains, textiles, paper, lumber, and cider, fueling the industries that allowed an emerging nation to grow and prosper. Many smaller ones, called ghost dams, do not always appear on maps and inventories. No more than a few feet tall, they were built on small farms and homesteads to create ice ponds for refrigeration. All these barriers are ubiquitous, such a familiar part of the landscape that we barely notice them. And all of them fragment their waterways, hinder fish passage, accumulate sediment, and otherwise diminish water quality.

I knew that in recent years there had been a nascent crusade to remove these dams, to drain their impoundments, to restore the flow and resume the connections of their waterways. The questions around which barriers were maintained, which ones were allowed to breach, and which ones were dismantled entirely began to interest me more and more. The decisions and issues surrounding such decisions were ecological, economic, social, political—and human. Still water and running water affect us deeply and in deeply different ways, which is what motivated me to look more closely at these waterscapes and the work around them, and to understand the strategies and the spirit with which these rivers and streams could, ultimately, be restored and reconnected.

Figure 1. The lower reaches of the Wynants Kill in Troy, New York, remain scarred by industry.

From the Millpond to the Stream

> Much of what I know about integrity, constancy, power, and nobility I've learned from this river, just as I've learned the opposite of these things—impotency, fecklessness, imprisonment—by walking across the dam on Blue River, a tributary of the McKenzie, and by standing on Cougar Dam on the river's South Fork, another tributary. I stare at the reservoirs from the tops of these dams and see the stillness of the impoundments. The absence of freedom there.
>
> —Barry Lopez[1]

The first time I drove over the Wynants Kill in 2023, I missed it altogether. The creek was only about fifteen feet wide, barely noticeable, and the bridge spanning it just part of the straightaway on a desolate brownfield site. What caught my eye instead were the old, abandoned factory buildings, a series of stark cement silos, and the wide expanse of the Hudson River just beyond, a slab of chocolate-colored water on that late March morning. It wasn't until a mile or so later that I realized my mistake and turned around.

The Wynants Kill is a fourteen-mile-long tributary of the Hudson River. It is channeled through a narrow concrete strait where it flows into the river in south Troy, New York. To get to that small confluence by land, you park in a lot covered in gravel and strewn with cement rubble, walk through another area strewn with litter, a pile of old tires, and other trash, then through a thicket of brittle, dried Japanese knotweed. The concrete walls of the channel are about twenty feet high, though only about a foot of water is coursing along its floor now. A few of its panels are decorated with graffiti, and one of them has slipped out of place, resting at an angle on the floor of the creek.

Upstream a few hundred feet, the channel walls give way to a just nominally natural shoreline, but even here, old bricks, piles of rubble, and other bits of indeterminate industrial slag line the corridor of the waterway, while rusted pipes and iron bridgeways span the creek just above the surface of the water. How the creek flows and where it converges with the river offers a history of the city's industry—from the gristmills and sawmills of the eighteenth century to the glass factories and paper and textiles mills of subsequent generations, and in more recent history, steel factories, fuel plants, gas and oil distribution facilities, and a transfer station.

The story of Troy's industry is the story of water. The city is at the top of the navigable Hudson, and if the Wynants Kill supplied the power, the Hudson River supplied the transportation.[2] Flowing water was the technology of the day. The walk up the stream offers a timeline of that industry, or perhaps more accurately, a timeline of its decline. A couple of miles up the hill from the river is Burden Pond, dammed and formed in 1852 to manage the creek as a source of hydropower for the Burden Ironworks, the foundry downstream. Water from the pond flowed through a four-foot feeder pipe to the Burden waterwheel. Measuring some sixty-two feet in diameter, the waterwheel was the largest in the world and powered a robust nineteenth-century enterprise for the production of nails, horseshoes, and railroad spikes.

The wheel is long gone now. To get to its site you leave your car at the Speedway pit stop gas station and follow the path of the creek upstream, past a series of natural falls and cascades, past an area where the channel was rerouted and straightened, and past another dam some forty feet high, eighty feet wide. A tangled underbrush of vines, grass, and shrubbery takes you to a barely discernible old access road through woodlands of maple, oak, and poplar. A few antique stone foundation walls remain visible. Kick the dirt and leaves aside and you find lumps of pig iron, stumps of old telephone poles, corroded wires, piles of crumbling bricks, remnants of cast-iron piping, anchor bolts sticking out of the ground, bits of concrete slab, and lengths of rusted cable. The site where the gigantic wheel once stood, just downstream from Burden Pond, is a great crevice in the ground. Four silver maples grow there now.

When the pond no longer served as a source for hydropower, it became part of a bucolic urban park used for boating and fishing, ice skating in winter months. Today, it is shallowed with sediment, a combination of gravel, sand, silt, and clay. Mostly a marsh, some areas are mudflats, others thickets of cattails, phragmites, and scrubby willows. It's maintained, but littered with soda cans, sandwich wrappers, old tires, much of it probably trash from stormwater runoff. To get to the trails around it, you leave your car at the laundromat parking lot and climb over a guardrail. That said, the wetlands remain part of a nature preserve used by city residents, a place they can watch birds, feed the ducks, and picnic.

But if the banks of the Wynants Kill are a decrepit industrial corridor, the creek itself flows just a bit more clearly and continuously than it did twenty years ago—from the silted pond, past the site of the old wheel, over one remaining dam to the degraded shore and concrete spillway, and into the Hudson River. Attached to the walls of the channel, about fifty feet from the mouth of the creek, are two large metal anchor bolts, the only evidence of the six-foot metal Tainter gate once installed there. A radial arm floodgate used to control water, it had been used for nearly a century by industrial enterprises on the riverfront to monitor the flow of the creek. Where the creek finally meets the river, the confluence now creates a small flume of white wave and churning riffle, as though the two waterways are perpetually astonished to encounter one another here.

As the first barrier where the stream meets the Hudson River, the rusty gate, though long out of use, had remained in place, obstructing fish passage, blocking sediment, and otherwise impeding the creek's natural flow. On one of his monthly upriver patrols in 2013, John Lipscomb, longtime captain for Riverkeeper, the nonprofit environmental watchdog organization, had noticed discharge into the river from the site of one of the abandoned mill buildings. Lipscomb's title at Riverkeeper was patrol boat captain and vice president for advocacy, but he is more informally recognized as the eyes and ears of the Hudson River. He works from what he calls "a floating pick-up truck." It is, in fact, a Chesapeake Bay Deadrise workboat. And his vigilance is twofold: While he is on the watch for construction, illegal fill, and discharge, the very presence of the boat often itself deters bad behavior. In this case, it turned out the discharge was coming from a pipe connected to a sluiceway attached to the dilapidated gate.

In 2016, the barrier was removed—with funds from the New York State Department of Environmental Conservation (NYSDEC) through the Hudson River Estuary Program and additional support from the City of Troy, Riverkeeper, Cornell University's Water Resources Institute, and the U.S. Fish and Wildlife Service Program. The removal signaled an inaugural effort to remove outdated barriers in the Hudson River watershed expressly to advance fish passage. Soon after, hundreds of herring, their population in decline for decades due to habitat loss, were making their way upstream to spawn. American eel, white sucker, and yellow perch followed, migratory and resident fish that together play a key role in the ecosystem of the river and its tributaries.

In helping to reduce flooding, improving water quality, and allowing for natural sediment flow, removing barriers also creates broader ecological renewal. Such efforts are no small thing at a time when the character of the Hudson River is changing quickly and unpredictably, when its waters are rising and warming, and when nonnative species, plant and animal alike, further disrupt the river's established systems. The removal of the Tainter barrier was an early step in reconnecting tributaries with the Hudson River. As Lipscomb said, "We've been talking to the New York State DEC Estuary Program for years about their initiative to take down barriers for fish migration, and in May 2016, the city of Troy came down here, and it took a loader and a cutting torch, and the barrier that had been there for 85 years was gone."[3]

I scroll through the pictures of the Wynants Kill site that I have on my phone: Chain link from Rent-a-Fence surrounds the old factory buildings, roofs have caved in, and piles of industrial debris litter the entire area. A wide expanse of gray stone rip rap lines the shore on the Hudson River, an effort to stabilize its banks that would be better served by trees and shrubs, more effective in managing erosion. But I glance as well at another photograph sent to me by my friend Doug Reed from a recent visit he's made to the site. Doug is the founder of Hudson Basin River Watch, an aquatic ecologist, and a watershed educator committed to river restoration. He regularly visits reclaimed sites such as this, gathering data and teaching high-school kids about shoreline ecology, water quality, fish habitat, and insect life. In the picture, the biologists and students are wearing waders and combing through the dark waters of the creek as it churns through the narrow walls of the spillway. Above them, a bright ceiling of vines and leaves hanging over the walls captures the light of the spring day, and one can glimpse at the end of the tunnel a bit of shine from the Hudson River.

The image of the river and the light, the foreboding dark tunnel and luster of the water at the far end, is almost too obvious. Yet it speaks to the spirit of the project that brought about the transition of an industrial waterway to a free-flowing stream, from confinement to an open course, from shadow to light. Fish passage was restored—for a half mile, anyway—and a camera in the water captures the quicksilver flash of the herring coalescing with the glisten of the water as they find their way upstream for the first time in nearly a century. The project also signaled the start of a collaborative effort throughout the watershed to remove other antiquated barriers. But this stretch of the creek remains part of a brownfield site, legacy toxins likely remain embedded in the soil, and the concrete channel is hardscaping not entirely fish friendly: The concrete walls and floor of the channel are challenging to fish, which generally prefer waterways with varying speeds, riffles, softer edges, pebbled areas where they can take a rest. Herring are robust swimmers so many can get through, and eels have a way of slithering almost anywhere, but the hardscaping of the channel makes for a single swift stream, not unlike a moving sidewalk in an airport.

~

To be sure, not all barriers can be removed so quickly or easily. There is still a long way to go, but the work at the Wynants Kill is a good place to start thinking about streams and their dams. It's a first barrier dam, meaning it's the one on the tributary closest to the mouth of the river. Its dismantling was the first in a now continuing initiative to remove barriers, advance coastal resiliency, and improve aquatic habitat in the Hudson River watershed. As I found, it's not just the barrier itself that was easy to miss. Sediment flow, the water quality, the absence and presence of fish, and the degradation of habitat had all been overlooked for generations. And along with manmade barriers, the section of the stream between the mouth and Burden Pond has a series of natural falls, something else that makes it ideal to study fish passage.

Lipscomb has spent decades patrolling the river, testing water quality, identifying polluters and contamination sites, checking on the status of clean-up initiatives, exploring the condition of wildlife habitats. He knows the river and its shoreline intimately, and it's pretty obvious he's a realist. Yet when he speaks it is often with a sense of incredulity, both in tone and content. His disbelief tends to be relegated to two areas: what humans are capable of, and how the natural world can, sometimes, recover from those capabilities. Pragmatist though he may be, he remains susceptible to awe. In a short film about dam removal, when he's speaking of fish migration on the Wynants Kill, notwithstanding the ratty baseball cap, the two-day stubble, and the weathered river captain persona, his eyes soften, and his voice gets husky:

> Five days after it came down, they put a camera in the water, and there were herring coming up the Wynants Kill. They had

reached their spawning ground and they were going to fulfill their destiny. And when you think about what's happening in these migrations, is that these fish are born in the Upper Hudson. They had left when they were this big [gesturing two inches with his thumb and forefinger], years ago. And they came back on faith, driven by forces that are beyond all our understanding. And they found that fast water coming over the dam. And fast water to them says: A tributary! We want to go in there. We want to get above the tide, want to get away from the predators. So for eighty-five years, their parents, their grandparents, their great-grandparents, their great-great-great-grandparents, have been coming up and knocking on the door at that dam. Nobody home. . . . It's a wondrous thing to be involved in something like that. It was the first barrier in the history of the Hudson Valley removed expressly for fish passage. The dams were all built one at a time. They're going to come down one dam at a time.[4]

The Wynants Kill is only one of the sixty-seven tributaries in the Lower Hudson River watershed, an overall area that covers about 13,400 square miles from the Adirondacks to New York City. And an area—it should be noted—that is based on topography rather than any municipal or political boundaries. A good half of those tributaries are impeded by dams. Add them all up, and these tributaries are disrupted by some 1,600 inventoried dams, metal gates, and low-head dams that range from under a foot high to a twenty-five-foot drop, to taller, more commanding barriers constructed for hydropower. Add in those smaller ghost dams that have not been inventoried, and there may be over 2,500 such barriers. Their value in helping to power an emerging nation in the eighteenth and nineteenth centuries is indisputable, but their detriment to their waterways today is just as unarguable. Yet they are everywhere, sheathed in moss and crusted with lichen, or pitted with rain, weather, and time. Often, they seem to exist on the periphery, barely noticeable, overgrown with weeds and willows, choked with shrubs. Some are rushing with water, others barely look to be dripping.

As climate change continues to bring more rain, snow, and otherwise wet conditions to the American Northeast, the state of these barriers, their purpose—or lack of purpose—and their effect on waterways are increasingly called into question. Climate scientists are only beginning to understand new patterns of heavier and more extreme rain and snowfall in the Northeastern states and their subsequent impact on infrastructure: Winds are stronger, warmer temperatures make for greater rainfall, often on dry, hard land, and storms move more slowly and with greater force. More back-to-back storms are predicted. Hundred-year floods now occur every few years, and recovery time is compressed. Built with tolerances for the waterflow that was common a century or two ago, these antique structures with spillways now considered undersized are generally inadequate for the powerful surges, intensity, and frequency of today's heavier rains. In early 2025, the New York State Comptroller's office conducted an audit of high-risk dams across the state, finding that some twenty percent of the barriers were without an emergency plan, and of those, many were also lacking updated engineering assessments.

The last two centuries have seen changes in demographics, land use, and our ideas of the natural world. Remnants of early American infrastructure, most dams in the Hudson River watershed serve little function today; rarely do they serve as power sources or as reservoirs. Few are used for flood control, and we get our ice elsewhere. Most have outlived their intended lifespans. Their removal has become an ecological focal point. Dams bisect habitats and restrict biodiversity; they obstruct the migration and spawning of such species as blueback herring, alewife, eels, American shad, white sucker, smallmouth bass. And all of them, says George Jackman, senior habitat restoration manager at Riverkeeper, are "functional blood clots." The entire Hudson River watershed has a circulatory problem, he has said, suggesting that ecologists, along with the rest of us, "need to act as cardiologists to remove the clots—not singular cells, but massive cell systems." That is to say: Dams don't just fragment streams, they fragment entire ecosystems. Ghosts of capitalism in Jackman's view, their disadvantages now far outweigh their benefits.

Dams raise the temperature of impounded water, altering species' habitats. They can trap sediment, block nutrient flow, and create artificial flow patterns for the creek or river in question, all of which degrades water quality. Regarding the decline of our waterways, there are certain things we can't do much about: the arrival of nonnative species, power plants that suck in eggs and larvae, overfishing, pollution. But taking down dams *is* something we can do.[5] American Rivers, the national organization formed to protect and restore the nation's waterways, reports that eighty dams around the country were removed in 2023, reconnecting more than 895 upstream river miles across twenty-five states. It further reports that 30,000 more—out of 400,000—remain to be dismantled, no longer providing power or useful resources to their communities. A 2019 report by the Nature Conservancy to its one million members observed, "Removing obsolete or derelict dams gives rivers more access to natural features—like floodplains, wetlands, side channels and marshes—which can help: improve water quality; support healthier, native plant communities; enhance fish and wildlife habitat; create or enhance recreational opportunities; recharge important aquifers; and, in cases, reduce flood risks for communities."

The removal of dams in the Hudson River watershed began in earnest in 2016 when the Hudson River Estuary Program developed a grants program to advance coastal resiliency and aquatic habitats. Fran Dunwell recalls that it started with the agency's strategic planning process in 2015. A celebrated activist and widely recognized as a hero of river restoration, Dunwell was the Hudson River Estuary coordinator at the New York State DEC from 1984 to 2022. The living river—the life cycles of fish species, aquatic plants, river habitats, fisheries, and the ever-changing minutiae of estuarine ecology—has been her life's work. Although we tend to think of the Hudson as a free-flowing river, half of its 315-mile course, from New York Harbor up to Troy, is an estuary. That 153-mile stretch is famously known as "the river that flows both ways," or as the Mohicans called it, "Mahicantuck."

It remains a place where freshwater from tributaries converges with salt water from the ocean, and the pull of both keeps the brackish water churning. Water comes from both mountains and sea, running with a current and ebbing and flowing with the tide as well. Its composition, its sources, its substance, its movement, its direction are all complex, intermingled, and mutable. This may be a chaotic mix, but it's one that feeds aquatic biodiversity and one where life flourishes. Estuaries are fantastically productive ecosystems, and as a dynamic transitional zone, this one supports over 200 species of fish, both resident and migratory, and is an especially critical waterway for diadromous fish, those that spend their lives in both saltwater and freshwater. Diadromy itself is presumed to be an evolutionary strategy that evolved to safeguard juvenile fish in quieter freshwater from the predators and more powerful currents of the ocean: As the juveniles grow in strength and stature, they are able to navigate the more powerful sea waters.[6]

Over the years I had occasionally visited Dunwell in her office in New Paltz, but the estuary itself was her real workplace. Retired now and sitting at her kitchen table with me over a cup of coffee, Dunwell takes obvious pleasure in reconnecting with her past, and her eyes spark in reviewing the origins of this initiative. "The question," she says, "was what was the connection of dam removal to the estuary? In our strategic plan, everything had to connect in one way or another to benefit the estuary. The program had a focus on migratory fish species that use the estuary ecosystem for their life cycle." Herring, for example, play a key role in the health of ecosystems by recycling nutrients; spawned in freshwater, they return to the sea and spend a lifetime dining on plankton and fish eggs. Enriched by such marine nutrients, they return to their natal freshwater streams to spawn at the end of their lives. They leave some of those nutrients there in a cycle that provides essential ecological services to the waterways; when the cycle slows or ceases, those waterways become degraded.

"For the most part, that focus was anadromous species," says Dunwell. "Those fish, such as striped bass, shad, sturgeon, as well as river herring, that come in from the ocean to spawn in freshwater or tidal streams." But she adds that the steep inclines and waterfalls along the Hudson make it difficult for herring passage of any significant distance. The Hudson is different from most estuaries, which tend to be in more gently sloping terrain. Stripers and sturgeon spawn in the estuary, but the alewife herring go into streams where they are just as likely to encounter a waterfall as a dam. Thus it was hard to justify dam removal on any large scale based on economic importance to anadromous fish. "But we were also starting to think about American eel," she adds, "in part because we were developing a successful community science program around monitoring the eel as they come into the tributaries."

An estuarine species, American eels are vital to the food chain both as predator and prey: Their diet consists of invertebrates, small fish, frogs, crustaceans, and dead organisms, while eels themselves are on the menu of bald eagles. Eels are also catadromous, which means they come into the estuary and its tributaries to mature, then swim back out to the Sargasso Sea to spawn. In recent years their numbers in North America have been in steep decline. The consensus in the fisheries community was that the population drop, at least in part, was a result of degraded habitats, changes on oceanic drift patterns, and fragmented waterways—meaning the proliferation of dams, which break up freshwater habitats and prevent fish from getting access to the places they need to spread out and grow. Resourceful and tenacious, eels can find ways to navigate waterfalls and can use an entire stream as a habitat: Tributaries of the river can potentially provide many hundreds of miles of habitat, supporting thousands of the fish as they mature. But dams pose a problem, with each one reducing the number of eels that can make it upstream by 10 percent.

This is why the estuary program's education initiative—recruiting schoolkids up and down the Hudson's tributaries each spring to help monitor eel counts—could contribute to the science of American eel conservation. "That was a part of our strategic plan," Dunwell says. "Let's tie our education not only to helping kids understand the natural world but to having their community science actually contribute to the conservation. You wouldn't believe how kids form an emotional bond with the juvenile eels: easy to catch, easy to count, easy to release. And utterly adorable to children, strangely enough. And we were always trying to tie our education program to our scientific program, to our fisheries management program and to our water management program. So we started exploring the status of American eel." In its efforts to monitor eels, how many are coming into the Hudson, when, and where, the research federation made up of elementary and high-school kids has caught, counted, and released over two million eels since 2008. Their collections are made in only a handful of tributaries and the nets don't cover the full width of the stream, so that number represents only a small portion of the total number of eels that enter the Hudson River system.[7]

The focus in government agencies, Dunwell explains, tended to be "on species economically important, either for food or commercially important as sport fish, often catch and release. Or endangered species. And I think the feeling is that the eels could become endangered. So a lot of people are focusing on what we can do now to prevent them from falling off the cliff. When dams are brought down, each one is a victory." With all that in mind, the estuary program established a grants program in 2016, putting out a call to both private landowners and municipalities interested in dam removal to benefit migratory fish. The free study offered by the program included research into the cost of dam removal as well as assistance in grant writing. A town participating in the program would agree to move forward with efforts to obtain grant funding to remove the dam. The grants prioritized the first, second, and third barriers to eel passage upstream of the estuary, Dunwell explains, but because all dam removals benefit eels to some extent, wherever willing property owners and high-quality habitats were found, removals were funded.

The program raised awareness of derelict dams. The gate at the Wynants Kill that once served industrial purposes in an emerging city had become obsolete, but throughout the watershed, other dams clearly qualified for the study. With its seepage and leaks, water coursing through the limestone around it, the dam at Furnace Pond on the Fishkill Creek is a record of age, history, disrepair, vulnerability, and the frailty of human enterprise. The land lying behind the dam had been the site of an iron ore mine in the mid-nineteenth century, and when the mine ceased production, the crater in the ground was filled with water to form a ten-acre lake. The furnace just downstream, built for smelting in 1831, was dismantled, and its stones used to construct the dam in the 1880s. But if a dam once signaled the human impulse and ability to control the natural world, or at least to marshal its energy and force, this dilapidated structure speaks to the erosion of such efforts. Still, its preservation matters to local residents. They cherish the pond it creates. They take their kids to fish there, and on sunny spring weekends, they walk the trails around it or simply sit at its edge to take in some of its tranquility. Its stillness confers a sense of composure.

Just upstream is the McKinney dam that had breached through time and neglect, leaving behind a muddy floodplain bisected by a thin creek. But the mudflat, it turns out, served as an incidental seedbank as well. Within ten days of the breach, sprouts of new growth had cast an emerald green veil across it. The leafy sawgrass would be the starter for the new plant community of the emerging wetland. A year later, when the channel had established its own course, a team from NYSDEC paid a visit. In an effort to stabilize the sediment along the new channel, the agency planted some two hundred seedlings sheathed in tubing that worked both as individual greenhouses and protection from browsing wildlife. A couple of years later, the tubes are scattered amid the thicket of scraggly grasses and shrubs, and what was until recently a pond bed is now on its way to becoming a forest of native trees—of red, sugar, and silver maples, of river birch, white pine, and sycamore—with a narrow creek winding through it. At a time when hundred-year floods have become common, when the cycle of downpour and drought seems constant, the free-flowing creek and emerging floodplain capable of accommodating the rush of high water signal resilience.

Another centuries-old dam several miles to the north at Shapp Pond has been dismantled with intention and forethought. Heavy rains from Tropical Storm Irene in 2011 had caused the creek to swell, loosening stones in an already unstable foundation, and water began to flow beneath them, further destabilizing the entire structure. In the sedate prose of the engineer who came to inspect the site, some measure "must be taken to either stabilize or remove this dam before a catastrophic breaching occurs during high flow conditions." Stone by stone, then, concrete block by concrete block, the dam was deconstructed and the stream reconnected with its original channel. The concrete abutments on either side were kept in place, and today they read almost as a frame for the restored creek. The highwater mark of the old millpond remains on the banks, but the stream follows a free-flowing course, its sense of swift passage restored.

Some of these dams were built in headwater streams close to their sources. With higher elevations and cool waters that provide refuge for those species unable to tolerate warmer temperatures downstream, such areas are of vital importance. As climate change brings on more frequent and more intense rainstorms that can disturb downstream reaches, headwater streams can also help to renew organisms and organic materials, recharge groundwater supply, and restore habitats.[8]

The dam at Jamawissa Creek in Cortlandt, New York, is at the other end of the reach. A first barrier dam, the dam closest to the Hudson River, it was never part of any milling operation; both the dam and its pond were created largely for aesthetics on a sprawling Hudson River estate. That property now serves as a park and conservation area open to the public. The dam's proximity to the mouth of the stream brings its own set of concerns, an excess of silt and sedimentation. Left in place, this material slows and otherwise obstructs the current. It is also contaminated. Where it might be put—and how—after the dam is dismantled is a crucial question that has led to a protracted permitting process. While the narrative tracks that shift from private to public use of land, the removal of the dam and subsequent draining of its impoundment also reflect evolving standards of beauty in the natural landscape, from manicured gardens and reflecting pond to river and stream reconnected, and habitat for fish and wildlife species repaired.

If aquatic passage was the primary motive for dam removal for the estuary program, the time I spent on these four sites also revealed a catalog of social concerns. Human safety considerations range from flooding due to sudden dam failure, hydraulic dangers just below the structure, and the degradation of water quality due to algae blooms that proliferate in increasingly warm impounded water. Recreation, local land use values, economics, cultural heritage, historic preservation, and aesthetics are other human factors that figure in to decisions around dam removal as well. When you consider all this, along with the ecology of migratory fish, the growing sense of urgency around removing outdated barriers and reconnecting waterways makes sense.[9]

"Maintenance. Removal. Neglect." Scott Cuppett, a watershed program manager at Cornell University's Water Resources Institute and the Hudson River Estuary Program, states that these are the three basic options for these antiquated constructions. "If you truly care about what happens downstream, you'll remove the dam," he tells me when I reach him by phone. "Doing nothing is not a good environmental choice. Or you can ignore it until it breaches on its own. Or you can maintain it forever. Whatever forever means." When he pauses, it strikes me that these three options are the same ones we confront in so many of our endeavors.

Cuppett's commitment to stream restoration and resilience is rooted in personal history. He grew up in a small town outside of Johnstown, Pennsylvania, where cataclysmic dam failure seems to be the city's legacy. After heavy rainfall, the infamous flood of 1899 caused a dam breach, taking the lives of 2,208 people—though it would be a mistake to assume the tragedy had been caused simply by excessive rain. Then as now, flooding is not just a matter of torrential rainfall, but of human (mis)management, whether artificial channels, indifference to floodplains, undersized and clogged spillways, or earthen dams that are structurally inadequate in withstanding a sudden surge in water flow and volume. Here, crucial factors to the catastrophe were a derelict and cracked dam upstream and a riverbed that had been narrowed by slag from the nearby iron furnaces, a diminishment of width that made the river even more prone to flooding. In 1936, flooding from rain and melting snow demolished more than seventy-five buildings. Two dozen people lost their lives. And in 1977, when Cuppett was a child, heavy rainfall—twelve inches in ten hours—resulted in the failure of five dams. The subsequent flooding killed some eighty people in the city, with forty of those deaths attributed to dam failure. Some of those who lost their lives were members of Cuppett's immediate community, members of his family's church. "It's a memory I have that still pushes me forward removing dams," says Cuppett, "because I understand the implications and experienced that in my formative years."[10]

Maintenance, removal, neglect. The choices Cuppett spells out were clearly reflected in the sites I visited. I found myself drawn to them partly for the industry of old stones and mortar, for the calligraphy of lichen scribbled across the abutments, for the beauty intrinsic to the archeology of these old river enterprises. Their stories also reflect those ways in which we become attached to place and how we recognize the way landscape gives shape to our lives. While that effort to shape the natural world seems to be woven into our very beings, the natural world also shapes us. It is a reciprocal arrangement. Rivers, streams, ponds are the arteries that guide us, help us get our bearings, and find our way through things in our own cognitive mapmaking. On the authority of Herman Melville, water and mediation are wedded forever. Whether the waterways inscribed in our imaginations are free-flowing or impounded matters. High water and low water imprint differently on the human psyche. In his book *Blue Mind*, Wallace Nichols explores those ways in which humans are affected by being on, near, and around water, and suggests we build "our perceptual maps based on the sensory experiences we pay attention to in the world."[11] At a time when the management of our waterways is ever more crucial, it seems worthwhile to pay attention to those perceptual maps.

Lotic (moving) water and lentic (still) water have different flow patterns, different ecologies, different processes of chemistry; they operate within different systems. Lotic water contains more oxygen, and in flowing, it is clearer. Passing from headwater to mouth, its shifts in elevation and gradations of temperature allow it to nurture greater variation in plant and animal species. Lentic systems, standing water in anything from a vernal pool to a lake, have less diversity. Often a product of groundwater, lentic waters can be without a single, definitive source. Yet decomposing organic matter in their depths releases nutrients, allowing them often to act as reservoirs for aquatic vegetation. I'd like to think these two ecosystems have corollaries in the human imagination; these may be less quantifiable, but flowing and still water touch us in different ways.

Still water, whether in marshes, ephemeral pools, or lakes, invites reflection and repose. A centuries-old dam and its pond where we have gone swimming or fishing with our children may be indelibly scripted in memory. *Walden* may be a book about a pond, but it is also a book about time, solitude, community, work, a book about how to think, live, and be. It is just as Thoreau writes: "Over this great expanse there is no disturbance but it is thus at once gently smoothed away and assuaged, as, when a vase of water is jarred, the trembling circles seek the shore and all is smooth again."

Jean-Jacques Rousseau's famous Fifth Walk offers an evocative recollection of the lake where he "would slip away and go throw myself alone into a boat that I rowed to the middle of the lake where the water was calm; and there, stretching myself out full-length in my boat, my eyes turned to heaven, I let myself drift slowly back and forth with the water, sometimes for several hours, plunged in a thousand confused, but delightful, reveries which, without having any well-determined or constant object, were in my opinion a hundred times preferable to the sweetest things I had found in what are called the pleasures of life."

If still water quiets human agitation, the dynamism of the rivers, streams, and springs in lotic systems conveys ideas about continuity, progress, forward movement, the rush of time. Streaming water speaks to change, momentum, energy, even turbulence, all qualities as vital to our beings as tranquility and reflection. "We have an unknown distance yet to run, an unknown river to explore. What falls there are, we know not; what rocks beset the channel, we know not; what walls rise over the river, we know not. Ah well! we may conjecture many things." These are the words of John Wesley Powell as he looked ahead to sure danger and uncertainty before he set off down the rapids, chutes, and falls of the Colorado River in 1869.

Questions about what is static and what is dynamic are essential to human endeavor. A reflective pond and a swift river speak to contrasting facets of human experience: to holding back and moving ahead; to stillness and motion; to repose and action; to rest and movement; to passivity and force. Possibly even to silence and expression. And possibly even to restraint and freedom, impulses that are rudiments of human behavior. Writing about Thoreau's lifelong engagement with water, author Robert M. Thorson noted that "At Walden Pond, Thoreau was mainly interested in the purity and clarity of its isolated and stationary water. On his rivers, though, Thoreau was interested in the relentless flux of anything and everything through time."[12] When I sit in on a town board meeting where the possible demolition of a local dam is under discussion, I know I am hearing about environmental diligence, civic responsibility, funding sources, community perspective, and local history. But I am also witnessing a conversation about restraint and release.

Ebb and *flow* are the words we use to describe the cycles and patterns of ordinary events. And perhaps they echo concepts even more primal than that: *stop* and *go*, among the first words we learn to speak and read. Even as a writer (or probably anyone at all who is engaged in trying to figure out why things are the way they are), I know that to get anything done, I rely on both the quiet pooling of thoughts and impressions, a stillness that lasts over time, as well as the flow of a quick current and the sense of urgency that sets in sometimes to get a thought down, to put it into words before it's carried away. But I suspect we all count on the stillness of the pool and the rushing of the stream. Fixity and fluidity are conditions equally vital to human perception, behavior, experience. "Pond and river are complementary geometric forms: a circle and line, respectively," Thorson writes. I suspect these primary configurations endure in our own mapmaking brains. And we do, after all, call them *bodies* of water.

The dam, whether holding back or breached, is a mythic construct in the human imagination, an archetype in the subconscious. We seem to have an almost primal grasp of the contest between the weight of water and the weight of stone. The folktale about the small Dutch boy who put his finger in the dyke to prevent the sea from flooding his village resonates with ideas of resourcefulness, the power of nature, human frailty, action, inaction, inevitability. Something small stopping something big is always a story that engages us. And "water over the dam" is an expression we use to describe something irrevocably gone, ended, whether an experience, a belief, an opportunity, a choice, or a time that is lost to us forever.

And then there is the waterfall that so often accompanies the dam; the water surging over the spillway at Furnace Pond is usually a shining sheet of rushing water that conceals the edifice behind it, rendering the dam all but invisible; of course the waterfall engages the imagination. And I wonder, too, if our intuitive response to these stories and images has to do with our intuitive grasp of ideas of irretrievability. Our species has an inborn comprehension of ideas about the passage of time, and a working familiarity with finality may simply come with being human.

For the writer and activist Edward Abbey, the dam was a symbol of external forces that constrict the human spirit—social convention, religious dogma, federal regulations, or any number of other institutional interferences made by civil society. Abbey suggested that dynamite could be an acceptable remedy and that to demolish the dam was to liberate the natural progression of life itself. The former poet laureate poet Robert Hass believes that rivers are our ecological unconscious. In his 2013 essay "On Rivers & Stories," he writes that they "flow like stories and like stories they have a beginning, a middle, and an end. In between, they flow. Or would flow, if we let them." Hass suggests that commercial interruptions on television, like dams impeding rivers, pass "the human imagination through the turbine of a sales pitch to generate consumer lust."

I once impulsively volunteered to accompany a NYSDEC water management official on a site visit with a property owner who was considering dismantling a dam. My offer was rejected out of hand. I wondered at how my presence might be intrusive, then thought perhaps it was about water, land, ownership, possibly family ownership for generations. How we see ourselves as custodians of land, how we form attachments and connect to the places we live are sensitive matters, and maybe the NYSDEC guy just wanted a one-on-one meeting. I could be over-sentimentalizing a simple business meeting, but I hang on to the conviction that questions of land stewardship go deep, and when water is involved, they can go even deeper.

The metaphor of the dam breached can imply positive or negative experience—a flood of speech after a lengthy silence or the release of repressed anger or sadness or grief; or what is given and what is withheld.

If earth, stone, mortar, and the water they hold back are materials that offer us some microcosm for human construction, they also imply certainty, surety. And while viewing these waterways and their barriers as metaphors for human experience may seem to trivialize the subject matter, it is only human to find in the natural world ideas on how to be. Even the direct, lucid prose of John McPhee seems to support this idea: "The conservation movement is a mystical and religious force, and possibly the reaction to dams is so violent because rivers are the ultimate metaphors of existence, and dams destroy rivers."[13]

Here and elsewhere, I found that listening to writers, poets, and musicians was unavoidable. The appreciation for beauty and wonder infused the writing of Rachel Carson, who believed that writing about the systems of the natural world required both scientific accuracy and an awareness of the metaphorical and spiritual effect nature has on the human spirit. As she famously said during her acceptance speech in 1952 for the National Book Award in nonfiction: "The aim of science is to discover and illuminate truth. And that, I take it, is the aim of literature, whether biography or history or fiction. It seems to me, then, that there can be no separate literature of science." Sixty years later, her tribute to this reciprocity between human modes of perception and expression was echoed during a conversation at Poet's House in New York City between biologist E. O. Wilson and Robert Hass. Their exchange proposed that science is not purely analytical, nor poetry purely associative, but rather, two sensibilities that can coincide and inform each other. As their dialogue suggests, "All skilled human production depends on subtle networks of cognitive capacities and the ability to transition between them. Let us use all the tools we have as we seek truth about our place in nature and our stewardship of life on earth."[14]

Along with data points, experience, sensation, and memory form our knowledge of the natural world. Biologists have one way of explaining transpiration, that process in which plants release water into the atmosphere. But when poet Tony Hoagland writes of the social life of water, noting how

> Tree drinks rain and sweats out dew;
> Dew takes elevator into cloud;
> Cloud marries puddle;

he is offering a different view to this phenomenon. When Charles Darwin travelled, he took *Paradise Lost* with him, and in *The Autobiography of Charles Darwin*, a collection of his writing edited by his family, the scientist confesses that "if I had to live my life again, I would have made a rule to read some poetry and listen to some music at least once every week." Was the naturalist and biologist drawn to the pure pleasure around the sound of the words or was it the different avenues of perception he found in Milton that further informed his ideas about evolution? The poet Mark Doty writes that "Metaphor is a way of knowing the world," a way of getting to the truth of things, and "a way of paying attention, of reading the world."[15] Is this what Darwin was drawn to—metaphor as a language of understanding, a kind of parallel assessment of how nature (and we within it)—operate?

The composer and jazz clarinetist David Rothenberg comes to ecology through sound. When he drops a microphone into a pond, he is *listening* to the events beneath the surface, the sonic signals of the photosynthesis that removes carbon dioxide from the environment and replenishes oxygen. Aquatic plants take energy from the sun, and because they are underwater, he explains, the oxygen being released in the form of minuscule bubbles, though not often seen, can be heard. He records the sound, tuning into the unexpected rhythms that emerge for as long as the sun's effect is felt. The soundtrack of the pond takes in the faint sequence of delicate popping sounds interlaced with the soft hum of tiny water insects, dripping, a remote clicking, an indistinct ticking, other distant notes from undistinguishable sources. Their rhythms and frequencies vary, their patterns both normal and anomalous. "Do certain sounds suggest a healthier ecosystem?" he asks. "Are other signs warning signs of natural decline? How can we use this sonic information to better understand the world around us, so that we might save it and not imperil it?"[16]

In talking about the often strained relationship between the sciences and the humanities, it is Wilson who says, "We dream together and as a result the cultural products of human nature are vastly expanded and enriched."[17] And so, increasingly, I came to understand how the decisions we make around land use and stewardship reflect not only timely and urgent ecological concerns but also the deep and abiding associations we have with the land and water around us. Wilson calls this *biophilia*, believing that we humans have intrinsic connections to natural systems, an innate affinity for biological life across species and a sense of mutuality with the natural world that can animate the way we care for it. It seemed to me that if we are going to make intelligent decisions about this care, it is a good idea to recognize the sensibilities of both the millpond and the stream, the quiet water and the rushing brook.

A good place to begin might be in the history of these questions. Excoriating the Billerica millpond dam built in 1711 on the Concord River, Thoreau wrote in his journal in 1838, "Dam it up if you may, but dry it up you may not, for you cannot reach its source. If you stop up this avenue or that, anon it will come gurgling out where you least expected." A year later, he documented an upriver trip with his brother in his classic *A Week on the Concord and Merrimack Rivers*, speculating further on the purpose and efficacy of the dam and its impediment to the shad migration up the Concord. "Who hears the fishes when they cry?" he asked, anticipating the voices of environmentalists two centuries later who advocate for listening to the needs of other species.

"I for one am with thee," Thoreau wrote, "and who knows what may avail a crowbar against the Billerica Dam?" His antipathy to the dam extended to the fact that the impounded waters flooded the meadows upstream, preventing farmers there from cultivating hay and other crops. But the philosophical clash between the pastoral and the industrial perspectives failed to resolve itself easily in the writer's imagination. Thoreau never took up the crowbar. Emerging nineteenth-century technologies and the mechanics of new industry and engineering interested, even fascinated, the writer and forged ideological tensions with his convictions about the human need for nature and unfettered wilderness.

Questions of human intervention have a different urgency today. Whether out of acquiescence or apathy, the impulse to "let nature take its course" once had a logic; the forces of nature were once such that they could correct human error. The effect of human disruption on the natural world is no longer a matter of missteps and follies but of ongoing catastrophes, and such passivity has become obsolete, inadequate in a world in which we have altered the very character of the air, the atmosphere, the water, and the ground around us. Bill McKibben in *The End of Nature* informed us over thirty years ago that our sense of nature as something that exists independently of human enterprise, as something "eternal and separate," has been eroded. Letting nature take its course, a strategy that seems applied today largely for reasons of cost, human convenience, or indifference, has become an indulgence that is at best as archaic, inefficient, and irrelevant as an eighteenth-century gristmill and at worst a pathway to disaster.

My tour of these sites reminded me again of how landscape—and waterscape—help shape our ideas about history and preservation. Memory is intrinsic to the way we experience the natural world. Strong convictions about land stewardship and how best to address the increasingly frail state of our waterways often encounter the powerful antagonistic force of human nostalgia, our ideas of an idyllic past when our relations with landscape seemed less fraught. But nostalgia is a selective enterprise. My neighbors and I take pleasure in the quiet of Furnace Pond, finding its rural idyll an antidote to the noise and din of modern life just beyond the edges of the water and its woodlands; but really, this is just the scenery of the day. Our predecessors here two centuries ago would have known this as a sooty, smoking, loud industrial site, the earth torn up, the sky thick with dust from the mine and fumes from the furnace. Nostalgia isn't just selective, it's fantastically inventive. And identity—of the landscape as well as of human beings—is rarely fixed, just like the movement of water.

We have come to consider subtraction as well as addition in our current negotiations with the land around us, both rural and urban. Demolishing the Berlin Wall in 1989 may have been the most auspicious event in the recent geopolitical history of such efforts, but more recently and closer to home, disassembling outdated and divisive infrastructure has become increasingly commonplace. In urban plans across America, the removal of elevated freeways and interstates that bisect and fragment cities in favor of accessible pedestrian boulevards and bike lanes that rejuvenate communities has found new appeal; and in doing so, suggests a different and more gracious understanding of the public realm. Witness New York's West Side Highway, San Francisco's Embarcadero, and Portland's Harbor Drive. When President Joe Biden's Inflation Reduction Act was passed in 2022, funds were designated for deconstruction as well as construction; city planners in downtown Milwaukee, for example, could consider replacing an interstate overpass bisecting the downtown area with a walkable boulevard. New urbanist John Norquist, a longtime advocate for such projects, has observed that the teardown movement can enhance economic recovery, neighborhood connectivity, property values, air quality, and human health.[18]

We are an infrastructure species, distinguished by our impulse to build. A 2017 study estimates that the material habitat that humans have created in roads, cities, rural housing, the active soil in cropland, and so forth, at 30 trillion tons, is some five orders of magnitude greater than the weight of the human beings that it sustains.[19] As we are called upon to address failing infrastructure, part of that process may lie in finding ways to restore natural systems, to recognize and support natural networks, whether they are migratory pathways, wildlife corridors, or unhindered waterways.

A dam may be among the most eloquent and practical expressions of that intrinsic human desire to stack up stones, one atop the other, that impulse we seem to have to use stones to leave a mark, a directional device as in the elegance of cairns, little constructions left in the forest, in the desert, and everywhere else people go for no purpose other than to say *I was here* or *go this way*, all of them small monuments to human presence. Besides, removing dams is expensive. And while it is almost always more expensive to repair and maintain them over decades, the human inclination to build usually prevails over the burden to remove.

But in the twenty-first century, absence may be as important as presence. Engineering landscapes probably comes with being human, but when the materials have been degraded over time and events and conditions of the natural world tend towards the extreme, de-engineering becomes an essential skill as well. What we build and what we tear down may be of like value, and our actions and negotiations with the natural landscape may be a matter of disassembly as well as assembly. We may be called upon for both kinds of enterprise, both kinds of imagination.

What is the opposite of a cairn? Can something that is gone, something that has been removed, also serve as a directive, as a navigational signal?

Can something that is absent keep us from getting lost?

Words whose meanings I once thought I understood came into question.

I have come to wonder about the use of the word *restorative*. Dam removal has invariably led to efforts to restore the stream bed, to restore the contouring of banks and native vegetation. Elsewhere in the American landscape, a restorative approach is finding new value: in beachfront areas where tidal marshes are restored to accommodate rising waters or on riverfronts where riparian plantings replace concrete walls and bulkheads. One journalist defined the trend in contemporary landscape design as being about "well-curated dirt."[20] But if it is easy to identify an ecology damaged by development, deforestation, habitat loss, or rising waters, it is more difficult to define restoration.

It's both a philosophical and ecological question. Is it a matter of returning landscape to its original wilderness? Or one of replacing soil and planting native trees and shrubs? Does it entail recreating natural habitats of native species and actually bringing in animal species that have fled? Restoration implies a return to some original state, but how does one identify that state? And in which particular moment of the past is it situated? Twenty years? Fifty? A century? And is such a return even truly possible? The greatest question may be how to consider restoring a landscape during a time when ecology, rainfall, and weather patterns are revised entirely and irrevocably. Historic standards are often irrelevant today, and efforts to recreate a bygone landscape are as tricky as revisiting any other realm of the past. Like so many other ideas that once seemed clear, the meaning of the word *restoration* becomes obscure on closer scrutiny.

Disturbance was another word that acquired ambiguity. As it is practiced today, ecology is increasingly accompanied by that prefix to describe the appraisal of disruption and recovery. While there is probably no geographic feature of the natural world that isn't subject to disruption and disturbance, these are constants in waterways, intrinsic to the dynamic character of any river or stream. That disturbance can generate robust health is yet another paradox. As the water rises and recedes in a floodplain, for example, new habitats can take shape and biodiversity flourishes. But it can be difficult today to draw clear distinctions between natural and artificial disruptions. Human interventions—such as hardscaping, channelizing, toxic contaminants, artificial flows, and fragmentation by dams—are not hard to identify and their effects are disturbing in the traditional sense of the word. Yet seemingly natural disturbances—changes in velocity, volume, flow, flooding, drought, the bends of a meander—are now also likely to have anthropogenic fingerprints on them. How to characterize disturbance, its causes, and whether it was help or hindrance were other questions.

As I visited these sites, of course, there was the water, always the water, whether a green creek flowing unchecked or a still pond reflecting the tree canopy and clouds overhead. I became mesmerized by the histories of these waters, by the stories revealed in their surfaces and depths, by their currents and quiet, by the habitats they offer, by the shifting species of plant and animal life on their banks. Over the course of months, I visited each of them at different points in their natural cycles, always finding something new about how we now find our way in the natural world. What is the difference in the way a blue heron finds its habitat in a still pond or near a running stream? I learned the answer to this, and much more.

To be sure, none of the stories of the Hudson River and its tributaries resemble the epic accounts of the waterways, impoundments, and gargantuan hydraulic engineering projects common to the American West, where a single river may be tasked with nurturing huge expanses of arid land, where colossal dams and vast reservoirs are engineered for municipal use and the cultivation of farmland in all but desert-like conditions. The dams here are not storage dams, which have the capacity to store water for timed releases, but run-of-river dams that form impoundments, allowing water to flow out just as it flows in, without scheduled outflow.

Still, I argue for the large meaning that can be found in small stories. Stewardship begins small, with property owners at the local level; it is a bottom-up rather than top-down enterprise. In the view of John Lipscomb, a ten-foot dam blocks fish just as much as a 500-foot dam. "You can prioritize dams and you can sort them a whole bunch of different ways," he says. "You can sort them by which is the most hazardous. You can sort them by which dam owner is most likely to let the dam go. Of course, from the fish's point of view is to say which dams are going to benefit aquatic life the most."[21] Likewise, herring can be confused by impoundments of any size. The hydrological signals they look for in flowing water are motion and current. Still water alerts them to the fact that they are not where they want to be.[22]

Those smaller stories also have a place for ephemeral streams, those temporary waterways that flow only after snowmelt or rainfall and whose paths may shift over time. More than 50 percent of American rivers begin in such transient streams. Usually unnamed and almost always unregulated, they are sometimes called "ghost waters" for their unpredictable and fleeting character. Yet these connections, passing and quick as they may be, are essential to the character of whatever follows, and by one estimation, the total length of streams in the United States is five times longer in high vs. low flow conditions.[23] Their "ephemeral connectivity" is vital to the water quality of lakes, rivers, and reservoirs downstream.[24] Not for the first time, I find myself encountering an ecological term—a word, a phrase, an idea—with broader relevance to the human experience. Finding *ephemeral connectivity* a useful reference to all those elusive encounters we can have with the world outside of ourselves, I realize again those ways in which the phenomena of the natural world help us understand our lives.

When you add up all the lesser tributaries and their multitude of barriers in the Hudson River watershed, you encounter an extravagance of impediments. Smaller dams on lesser waterways remain capable of affecting water stratification, sediment accumulation and flow, and the diversity of plant and animal life. They can bisect habitats and block the travel of nutrients. Many of them are dangerous to humans. Their widths and drop-offs may vary, but the character of moving water remains consistent. A four-foot dam with slow water can be as much of a barrier as a fifteen-foot dam with fast-flowing water. It is not always easy to follow the mathematics of moving water, falling water, speed, depth, volume, and velocity, and these can result in their own unexpected outcomes. As most humans discover at some point or other, degrees of impairment do not always align exactly with the measurements of obstruction.

I chose the four sites discussed here for the ways they articulate ideas about human need, desire, use, and intention in a time when our natural resources have become increasingly vulnerable: Visiting and revisiting these sites reinforced the decision to limit my scope to a single watershed. These sites speak to the changing economy of our waterways: Regardless of their scale, all dams begin as productive liquid assets, whether for hydropower, flood control, water storage, recreation, or something else. But over time, such benefits are called into question. Although it may be difficult to assign a precise cost value to sedimentation, damaged wetlands, and blocked fish passage, it is easier today to recognize dams as liabilities, public nuisances, and agents of environmental degradation.[25]

At times, the focus on a single area could seem confining, especially as there is a growing effort throughout the country to restore the natural flow of rivers and streams. By 2030, some 70 percent of dams in this country will be fifty years or older, aging and inadequate to meet the conditions of a changing climate.[26] The Penobscot River in Maine has 113 dams, many under review for removal. The future of the nineteen dams on the Charles River in Massachusetts is under question. In Pennsylvania alone, ten dams were taken down in 2022.

The national organization American Rivers, founded to protect the country's waterways, aims to remove 30,000 defunct dams by 2050. It has kept a national inventory of dam removals: from 1912 to 2023, 2,119 dams in the US have been dismantled, with the highest numbers in 2017 through 2019. Each year, the organization updates a database on its website of the number and location of dam removals across the country. In 2023, eighty dams in twenty-five states were removed, reconnecting more than 1,160 river miles. When the two dams on the Elwha River in Washington were removed in 2012 and 2014, the full length of the forty-five-mile long river was again open to habitat and passage for salmon and trout. And in 2024, the Klamath River Renewal Corporation completed the removal of four hydroelectric dams in Oregon and California, restoring over 400 miles of habitat and clearing migratory pathways for steelhead trout, salmon, and other native fish in what is the largest dam removal project in American history.

Still, there was value in staying regional, within the boundaries of a single watershed—and in that watershed, only a few tributaries. How else, I wondered, is it possible to write about a place? Digital technologies and the Global Positioning System (GPS) have collapsed our sense of space and geography, and online portals increasingly offer the perception of access. The internet allows us to be anywhere, anytime, as the conceit goes. But knowledge and understanding of a place is not a virtual enterprise. Loving a place expands it, extends it, and increases our understanding of it. Physical presence allows us to learn the textures, the rhythms of a place. Time is a factor: I came to know these places in different seasons, over years. At one site the dam breached slowly, then all at once, and its pond was drained in a matter of hours. At another, once the dismantling was planned it was a matter of years of site work, sediment management, obtaining permits, construction bids, and restoration design before a single section of concrete was removed. A permit for removal might have been involved. Or not.

For each site, there was always the question of *before* and *after*, two words central to how we recall and evaluate almost any experience. Here it was before the flood and after. Before the drought and after. Before and after the summer heat, the winter freeze, before the beaver pond pooled, after the sycamore and willow saplings were planted.

In *A Literature of Place* Barry Lopez writes:

"Over time I have come to think of these three qualities—paying intimate attention; a storied relationship to a place rather than a solely sensory awareness of it; and living in some sort of ethical unity with a place—as a fundamental human defense against loneliness. If you're intimate with a place, a place with whose history you're familiar, and you establish an ethical conversation with it, the implication that follows is this: the place knows you're there. It feels you. You will not be forgotten, cut off, abandoned.

As a writer I want to ask on behalf of the reader: How can a person obtain this? How can you occupy a place and also have it occupy you? How can you find such a reciprocity?

The key, I think, is to become vulnerable to a place. If you open yourself up, you can build intimacy. Out of such intimacy may come a sense of belonging, a sense of not being isolated in the universe."[27]

I came to know these four sites pretty well. Two are close to my home. Each has its own particular story, geography, ecology, texture. I sometimes tried to keep my thinking, my research confined to a single site. That was rarely successful. Their stories invariably converged. The son of an eighteenth-century farmer in Beekman established a mill several miles north in Hibernia—same watershed, different tributaries. Ecologists from NYSDEC would talk about two or three of these sites in a single sentence. The facts of these places flowed in and around each other, and trying to organize my notes was sometimes like trying to file water itself. Which made sense. This enterprise, after all, is about how things connect.

Somewhere in the course of this research, it became clear to me that the process itself was beginning to reflect its subject. Barriers seemed impassable, obstructions unsurmountable. At times I found myself inundated by information; other times its path was more quiet, manageable. I was prevented from seeing an engineer's report on one dam, and photographs filed in the local historical society of another seemed weirdly difficult to find. There was a guy in a pick-up truck who was happy to take me to a pond I wanted to visit, but he was disinclined to let me get out and have a look at the water, the sedge on its banks, the spot where it was fed by mountain streams. And even George Jackman, Riverkeeper's senior habitat restoration manager, ecologist, activist, and dam removal czar—the human embodiment of his life's interest and passion—responded to my phone calls and emails with intractable silence for weeks at a time. Yet when we finally connected, his thoughts, descriptions, recollections, and predictions poured forth in a cascade, a torrent, even, with multiple sources and tributaries. He can be astonishingly clear in his use of language, as when he cites data concerning river ecology and Hamlet's soliloquies in the same sentence. But at times, a bit murky: Once when we were trying to set up a meeting, he told me, "I'm coming at ten, but you'd better meet me at ten thirty in case I'm late." I wondered sometimes if investigating these sites was itself a tutorial in impediment and deluge. Or perhaps it was simply that phenomenon of finding one's subject of interest suddenly reflected in everything, everywhere.

The words used to tell the story presented their own choices. There is little difference between a creek and a stream, but when does a pond become lake? Definitions here can be as fluid as the water itself; area, depth, the penetration of light, the thermal layers of water, and the species and density of the aquatic plants growing there all figure into it. Although there are no consistent measurements or classifications, there is general agreement that a pond is determined by the shallow depth that allows light to reach the sediments of its bed. Often, though, it is just a matter of human use and perception, and the words are used almost interchangeably. It seems fitting that a body of water that summons such reflection is itself difficult to define precisely.

Names are just as variable. Some of these creeks, streams, and impoundments are known by the English adaptations of words used by indigenous populations. Others are known by the function they served in commercial enterprises. Others are known by their old Dutch names. And others still are identified by the names of the property owners, both past and present. Often these names change over time, just as different people may use different names at the same time. I have made the decision for two reasons here to call Furnace Creek in Cortlandt, New York, *Jamawissa Creek*, the name used by the indigenous Lenni Lenape meaning "place of small beaver": to call it Furnace Creek could cause confusion with an impoundment along a different tributary to the north called Furnace Pond. *Jamawissa* is also the name used by some of those involved in its restoration, here a process broad enough to include a return to old idioms. All these names can be as slippery as rocks and water, as fluid as the streams they identify. Even calling the pond an *impoundment*, a clinical and neutral term, is a linguistic maneuver that seems to emphasize ideas of restriction and restraint over tranquil reflection and beauty; *impoundment* can refer to basins of wastewater produced by coal mining just as accurately as it does to a shimmering millpond.

Add to all this that *dam* is never an easy word to use. In fact, it is a terrible word.

River, creek, course, stream, flow, torrent, tributary, estuary.

The language of water sounds as though it should, fluid and musical, with long vowels and rolling *r*'s. With its single short vowel and hard consonants, *dam* is a word that goes nowhere. It is not a sound that moves but a sound that stops. Which is to say, it, too, sounds as it does. If it were possible to find my way around this word, the way water might, that is what I would do.

Each of these four dams serves as a basic point of contact for exploring the interplay of human construction—earth, mortar, stones, water. We have an affinity for how these are arranged. There are so many things we build—houses, office buildings, bridges, roads—but a dam's purpose makes it a more elemental edifice. Whether we are aware of their presence or not, dams and their components define, in visceral and palpable ways, how we take up residence in a given area. There is something essential in their stories about the coinciding of human enterprise and natural systems. A dam once built to harness water to power a mill may now say little about shelter, accommodation, transportation, or human community, but it still speaks to essential concerns about natural forces, human need, and material structure.

The stories of Wynants Kill, Furnace Pond, Fishkill Creek, McKinney Pond, Wappinger Creek, Shapp Pond, Oscawana Park, and Jamawisssa Creek all address fundamental truths that exist when human endeavor and natural systems confront one another. At a time when our relations with the waterworld are imperiled, their varying currents are worth following.

Figure 2. Both the dam at Furnace Pond and the area around it continue to leak.

The Impoundment Preserved

Furnace Pond Dam

> If you are against something, you are for something.
> If you are against a dam, you are for a river.
>
> —David Brower[1]

A collection of rocks sits on the shelf below my office window. One is turquoise in color, its face rounded but with sharp edges. Another is dark grey, with streaks of the same vivid blue, but with pitted and serrated sides. A third is a deep eggplant purple, shiny and smooth. It's all slag, each stone its own amalgam of impure materials separated from iron ore during the smelting process. The rocks come from a huge pile of the stuff, dumped feet away from an old iron blast furnace built in 1831, when mining was the prevalent work in this part of the Hudson Valley. Iron ore deposits were found in the area in the early nineteenth century and the local economy shifted from farming to industrial mining and smelting. Forests were logged, the wood burned in pits to produce the charcoal needed to keep the newly built furnaces smoldering. Until this furnace was dismantled some fifty years later, the iron smelted there was used to make swords and cannonballs—some used during the Civil War.

The slag is among those phenomena best observed from a distance. At a certain angle, sunlight catches its glisten through the fallen leaves, which makes a kind of sense because the glittering rock is the understory of this place. It looks like nothing more than a pile of moldy oak and maple leaves, but brush them aside and you see the molten rocks, some of them nothing but pebbles, others the size of melons; some smooth turquoise or amber, others pockmarked and pitted by decades of rain and weather.

Moss and lichen have become attached to others. Nearby are other vestiges of nineteenth-century industry—a corroding iron sluice, crumbling stone foundations, a stone and concrete footbridge in disrepair. Mining continued until the late 1800s, when ore deposits were found elsewhere in the country, and the mines in Dutchess County were closed. The crater of the mining pit and the area around it were filled with water, and cement, bricks, mortar, and stone blocks taken from the old furnace were used to build a dam that formed the ten-acre Furnace Pond.

Today, that pond is part of a 500-acre town park. It is fringed by woods of white pine and hemlock, maple, oak, ash, and hickory and ringed by walking trails, from an old access road to lesser footpaths that intersect here and there with barely discernible deer paths. Even its name echoes with incongruity. *Furnace Pond.* It evokes both the ascendance of scorching flames and the depths of cool, still water. The very premise of the place is at odds with itself, and especially so at a dam where water streams between the stones of its downstream face, through fissures in the adjacent sluice pipe and beneath its banks on either side. A century and a half after its construction the dam means to hold the water back, but it's doing the opposite.

Just upstream, the Fishkill Creek feeding the pond runs fast through a rock gorge. A natural trout stream, it churns with whitewater, but when it reaches the pond, it quiets, and sediment clouds the water. The scars of industry have long been erased, though an old newspaper article I've found states that depth readings of the water have located one small area of 106 feet, a vestige of the old mine shaft. Even in months of drought, when the pond bed is mostly dry, I've never seen evidence of this. Still, it may lie beneath the bit of water that is always left there even during the driest days, and I've heard the locals go back and forth on this. Speculations about its depth and history seem in keeping with the reflective kind of thinking the pond summons.

"The pond invites the eye below the surface," historian Leo Marx wrote.[2] He was referring to Thoreau at Walden Pond, but he may as well have been speaking of any of us who have ever been drawn to thought at the edge of quiet water. Through a scrim of trees, from a distance, Furnace Pond can appear to be a flat sheet of silver shine, but get up closer to it and its color can vary from an opaque verdant jade on a spring day to dark, inscrutable granite on a winter morning. At water's edge, though, one can see clearly to the bed of decomposing leaves on the pond's floor. After a heavy rain has stirred up the sediment, it might be coffee-colored sludge, though the overcast sky a day or two later can give the water a cool, gray cast. The view to water is, by nature, mutable. Water changes its color by the time of day, by the season, by the quality of light. It changes with one's perspective, close or distant, or whether one is looking into it or across it. Our impressions and perceptions of water are as capricious as the substance itself, and looking at water reminds us that things are never static. While it may be possible to go through life forgetting this fact during events and circumstances of consequence, when we look at water, it is impossible not to grasp this.

Small wonder, then, that the very word *reflection* has double meanings, referring both to the image cast back to us, but also to the effort to think more deeply about something. In his reveries in *Walden*, Thoreau called the lake "a landscape's most beautiful and expressive feature. It is Earth's eye; looking into which the beholder measures the depth of his own nature." And if the mirage of the double image takes us back to ourselves, it also shows us our place in things, often in time as well as in place. The light on the water or a ripple on its surface may situate us just a bit differently. In his poem, "For Once, Then, Something," Robert Frost, on looking into the well, glimpses something: a drop of water falls from a fern

> . . . and lo, a ripple
> Shook whatever it was lay there at the bottom,
> Blurred it, blotted it out. What was the whiteness?
> Truth? A pebble of quartz? For once, then something.

It could be one or the other, something small, something elusive, a revelation, or perhaps both. Meaning is elusive.

The reflecting pool, the site of the inward gaze, is a convention of the human psyche. Narcissus may have been looking only for himself in the reflection, but the liquid image invariably gives us not just ourselves but whatever is around us: the sky, a streak of cirrus clouds, the faded green boards of the boathouse, the canopy of the forest. Gaston Bachelard was a twentieth-century French writer and philosopher concerned with how the human imagination enters into exchanges with the material world—with domestic space, with buildings, with landscape, with fire. And with water. And how patterns of human thinking and feeling are woven with those of the physical world. Bachelard allows that a pool brings the imagination to life; that deep water offers "a deepened perspective on the world and ourselves. It allows us to hold ourselves at a distance from the world. In the presence of deep water, you choose your vision; you can see the unmoving bottom or the current, the bank or infinity, just as you wish; you have the ambiguous right to see or not to see. . . . A pool contains a universe. A fragment of a dream contains an entire soul."[3]

Bachelard suggests that water returns to us a more natural image of ourselves; and that some essential quality of human character is lost in the bright clarity, rigid geometry, and sharp edges of a mirror. If water serves as a looking glass, it is one with uncertain depth, surface movement, and varying light. Lucidity and obscurity shift towards and away from one another; it could be a branch one spots beneath the water or an Eastern water snake. One does not dream so much with objects, Bachelard suggests, but with substances; the human imagination participates with water in a way it cannot with a square of glass.

It is with reason, then, that reflecting pools are common to commemorative architecture. The Taj Mahal in Agra, India, the tomb built by Mughal Emperor Shah Jahan to honor his cherished wife, is preceded by a long reflecting pool that re-envisions the materiality of the marble chamber, recasting it as fluid rather than solid, and in so doing, suggests all the transience in human feeling, thought, and existence. Nearly half a mile long, the reflecting pool in Washington, DC, is anchored at each end by the Lincoln Memorial and the Washington Monument and invites visitors to consider their place in the shimmering continuum—and uncertainties—of American democracy. And when architect Michael Arad spoke of the twin one-acre reflecting pools he designed for the 9/11 Memorial in Lower Manhattan, he repeatedly used the phrase "absence made visible." Sited in a grove of swamp white oaks and conforming to the footprints of the vanished towers, the pools offer guests a sanctuary, a retreat, a serene view of an unfathomable void.

By its very nature, a reflecting pool invites thought, and it is hard to object to any aspect of the natural world that asks human beings to quiet themselves. That's not a small thing. We once took a family vacation to the Grand Teton Mountains in Wyoming when I was eight or nine. Jenny Lake is a thousand-acre glacial lake created some 12,000 years ago and contained now by the moraine, the soil and sediment left behind by the glacier. My father took my sister and me trout fishing on the lake, and I remember sitting in the small boat and unspooling the reel. I tried to imagine the fishing line drifting out farther and farther through the wide water into a depth and distance far deeper and greater than anything I could see, and both the water and the nylon line seemed never ending. That morning on the lake was an introduction to the idea of infinity, something that had been abstract to me until that moment; even for a child, quiet water can lead to unexpected considerations.

I remember, too, summer mornings a few years later spent with a childhood friend on her family's pond. We'd get in an old rowboat and paddle around aimlessly and artlessly. With greater nerve and better rowing skills than me, she would maneuver us perilously close to the dam. My terror would grow with each stroke, as I was certain an undetected current in the pond would sweep us over the concrete edge to the rocks below. Our idyllic summer mornings were undercut—and enhanced as well—by the sensation of impending disaster. That experience, I know now, was an early primer on that alliance of beauty and danger that we humans seem to find so appealing.

The effects Furnace Pond has on the human psyche are not so different. Thoreau wrote in *Walden* of the composure conferred by his beloved pond, calling it a "perfect forest mirror."

> "Nothing so fair, so pure, and at the same time so large, as a lake, perchance, lies on the surface of the earth. Sky water. It needs no fence. Nations come and go defiling it. It is a mirror which no stone can crack, whose quicksilver will never wear off, whose gilding Nature continually repairs; no storms, no dust can dim its surface ever fresh;—a mirror in which all impurity presented to it sinks, swept and dusted by the sun's hazy brush."

My neighbors at the pond probably don't need an American transcendentalist or a French philosopher to tell them why they are there. Or that they are choosing their visions. They just love to walk around its edge. Its language shifts continually. In April, it seems to be a wide, brimming lake, but on dry summer days, it is a stagnant and shallow pond. I've heard the locals call it both *lake* and *pond*, and its shifting identity reminds me of how limnologists have had trouble drawing a clear distinction between the two. But if it's hard to catalogue water precisely, I know my own equilibrium often depends on my frequent walks around it, and sometimes nothing more than the shine of the water glimpsed through the scrim of hemlocks and white pines sets me right. Other times it is simply the sight of the pond brimming and its sense of sufficiency, of there being *enough*, that supplies a sense of fullness I may have been missing that day. Whether it is a mother pointing out to her young daughter the reflection of a blue

The Impoundment Preserved | 33

heron skimming its way low over the water's surface or a boy gazing into the water into which he has just thrown his fishing line, quiet water calms human agitation.

"A lake carries you into recesses of feeling otherwise impenetrable," William Wordsworth wrote in his *Guide to the Lakes* in 1810, and sometimes it is nothing more than the random biotic flotsam of the day that takes us to such recesses. In fall, the tinseled light scattered across the surface of the water collides with the shine of golden leaves strewn there as well. A month later, in November, a thin sheet of ice forms on the surface each night, then melts over the course of the next day. Indiscriminate geometric configurations form as the light and shadow across the water shift, affecting the water temperature just so slightly. But even in winter months, the frozen surface of Furnace Pond can invite conjecture; if not a mirror, it offers a more enigmatic diagram. In early January, when the temperature is just over thirty degrees, its surface is in part frozen, in part thawed, depending on the slant of sunlight and the currents beneath the surface. Myriad designs emerge—the deep green of the still water, and where that has frozen, the slate gray of ice, and where the sun has not yet hit that ice, patches of snow. Elsewhere, frozen air bubbles dot the surface in a random composition, while inky stress cracks and fissures embellish it in dazzling starburst patterns. Later in the season, as the ice melts and water pools on its surface, a choreography of clarity and opacity appears. Water finds its own assorted ways to record the changes in temperature, and somehow, this arrangement of disparate designs reads as an integrated whole. More than once, I have tried to sort through my own jumbled thoughts on a winter walk around the pond, imagining the possibility of my own mixed thinking finding some similar resolution.

When no longer in service to generate hydropower, dams are generally left in place, whether for flood control, irrigation needs, or fire suppression or because they are a reservoir and a water source. None of these come into play at Furnace Pond. Rather, the dam structure and the pond behind it have been preserved for less quantifiable reasons—scenic vistas, walking trails, and quiet pleasure. These, too, serve a function, and while definitions of beauty may be particular to each of us, I suspect a still pond is among the few universals.

And yet. Quiet water can stagnate. Still water can become dead water. Like many such dammed ponds, Furnace Pond has created its own sediment trap, and some aggregate of clay, silt, sand, gravel, and organic material has collected here, especially at the north end. In dry, hot summer months, its character is sluggish. Torpid bodies of water also have a place in our perceptual maps, and as an advocate for ambiguity, Bachelard believed that the imagination came to greatest life when confronted by duality and contradiction. "Water, the substance of life, is also the substance of death," he contended.[4] Suggesting that the imagination responds to putrid water with the same primal immediacy with which it responds to shimmering reflective pools, he assures us that nothing evokes death quite like water; and that the universe contained within the pool includes mortality, Stygian depth, and darkness with undertones of ultimate obscurity and silence.

Ecologists have a more technical view of dead water. Over the decades, Furnace Pond has shallowed and its water has become increasingly stratified, the term of art for the layering of water at varying temperatures. Cold water is denser than warm water and thus lies beneath it. Consider the experience of treading water in a pond in summer: One's legs are noticeably chillier than one's chest. During the winter and early spring, the temperature of the water is more uniform, with thermal stratification usually beginning well after the spring ice melt. As the days warm and the sun gets hotter, the surface water becomes warmer. Wind may mix up the layers, but as the days become hotter, the surface water warms up enough so the difference in temperature is significant.

By June, the surface water has become so warm it no longer mixes with the cooler water below. In the fall, the process is reversed, with the surface water cooling and wind mixing up the different layers. The period of stratification refers to what happens between those two seasons, that period between the two seasonal turnovers. In the Northeast, it is roughly from mid-May until late September. With climate change and warming temperatures, however, such stratification begins earlier, ends later, and thus lasts longer. With less turnover, the oxygen in the deeper, denser, cooler water remains diminished, which in turn can lead to toxic algae blooms and fish die-offs. If the water freezes over without that oxygen being replenished, aquatic organisms are likely to suffer even more, making for a biological wasteland. Not surprisingly, such water is often referred to as a "dead zone." Or, in Bachelard's words, "silent water, somber water, stagnant water, unfathomable water, so many material lessons for a meditation on death."[5]

Add to warming temperatures an increased nutrient load from human activity, and the opportunity for dead zones grows. In summer months when the water level is diminished, debris collects at the dam: sticks and logs from spring storms, a tangle of fishing line, trash from a picnic the previous summer, a plastic water bottle, a pink glove. Other forms of waste are less visible. Sunlight, slow-moving water, and nutrients such as nitrogen and phosphorus, byproducts of fertilizer, urban wastewater, septic sludge, emissions from cars and power plants, industrial waste, and animal manure are the key ingredients to harmful algae blooms that can be toxic to aquatic species. All of these cause disruptions in the flow of water and sediment, whether it is along the thirty-three miles of the Fishkill Creek or the 2,340 miles of the Mississippi River. The algae blooms in the Gulf of Mexico are a direct result of the nutrient overload in the latter, which carries 140 percent more nitrate than it did a century ago.[6] In a warming climate algae blooms flourish, and even the reflecting pool at the Lincoln Memorial has been drained for such blooms and parasites.

No surprise that a 2004 master plan for my local park had advocated for dam removal. Twenty years later, though, the twenty-five-foot-high dam at the south end of Furnace Pond continues to keep all this in place. Built on bedrock covered by a thin veneer of soil, it has a spillway about sixty feet long. It has a sloping, concrete face on its upstream side and pointed stone masonry downstream. On a warm spring day, the water coursing over the spillway conceals the stones on the dam's downstream face, but during dryer summer months, they are visible, polished smooth by generations of rushing water, some blanketed with moss, others tinged a rusty hue from the mineral-rich water. The sheer curtain of water falling over the spillway is constant, but a thinner stream of water rushes through a break in the rocks at the base of the dam. Other torrents are pouring out from the bedrock just below the dam's eastern abutment. The water follows alternative courses beneath and around the spillway, carving channels through stone and dolomite and surging through the dirt and leaves in more improvisational routes. Even in dry months, the constant trickle of water and the continuous dripping attest to the structure in decline. The impression of instability one gets from looking at the downstream face of the dam is reinforced by sound; even when there is no water passing over the spillway, it is easy to hear the water seeping through the bedrock near the abutment, streaming through the channels it has carved in the dolomite and limestone.

To be sure, seepage comes naturally to dams. It is in the character of impounded water to search out the path of least resistance, whether that is in the structure itself, through the foundation, or on the embankment. But with its cracks, crevices, and eroded embankment, this dam has become destabilized, and for over two decades the town has faced questions of how to maintain, repair, and otherwise restore the deteriorating structure. The 2004 master plan questioned the integrity of the dam, noting as well that the pond was silting in, and recommending that "removing the dam and restoring Fishkill Creek to its historical path may be the most ecologically and financially sound option for Furnace Pond." In the process, the plan suggested that upstream reaches of the creek that had been straightened and channelized be restored to their previous meanders.

The town had also considered dredging the pond in the early 2000s to remove collected sediment and other debris, aerate the water, and otherwise enhance circulation and upgrade water quality. But then, as now, dredging would be required to conform to DEC directives, the process including evaluation of possible toxins embedded in the sediment and consideration as to whether it should be buried in an immediate spoils area or trucked elsewhere for disposal. Like the pond itself, the project stagnated. When the Hudson River Estuary Program initiated its grants program for dam removal in 2016, it offered towns in the watershed a free study of both their dams and the costs of removal. Towns choosing to participate in the program would be asked to agree to move forward with applying for grant funding if dam removal were to be recommended. Wary of relinquishing the recreational benefits offered by the pond, Union Vale opted to solicit resident opinions, a decision that has helped to delay for another decade any clear path forward for repair or removal.

Furnace Pond is only a few miles south of Pray Pond, which is where the Fishkill Creek starts its thirty-three-mile passage to the Hudson River, and its dam is one of twenty-six known barriers in its watershed. In a world of greater reason, order and logic, it might make sense to begin with the first barrier dam, then move upstream sequentially, removing one dam after the other, opening fish passage in a logical progression from mouth to source. But dam removal isn't determined by some accepted metric. Rather, it is site specific and tends to happen when and where it can, the dismantling determined by the condition of the structure, public safety, community sentiment, local politics, funding, and the general will and wherewithal to do it.[7] This can seem counterintuitive, even irrational, but there may also be something hopeful about it. The truth is, you don't always have to start at the beginning. Or sometimes, the beginning isn't what you thought it was. Either way, when it comes to taking down a dam, you very easily might start at the beginning, the middle, or the end.

Wherever such removal begins, it almost always serves fish passage, whether those fish are resident species or diadromous fish that migrate between fresh and salt water. "The reality is that you can't always begin removal on a stream with the first dam," John Waldman tells me. "And that brings us back to the overall health of the river." Waldman is a fisherman, author, advocate for aquatic conservation biology, and professor at the City University of New York. My own tutorial with him had begun on my drive to visit him at his Queens College office, a journey that was unexpectedly analogous to what some aquatic species go through to reach their eventual destination. There was the swift river of morning traffic on the Long Island Expressway, a missed exit, and some quick and sudden lane changes. Once I pulled off and found the campus entrance, I needed to produce credentials to get a parking pass, then found that the college lanes and avenues were not identified clearly. I circled the area a couple of times before I finally made my way to a vast underground garage. Even when I finally found the science building, it took a few tries to find his third-floor office, which was off a narrow hallway reached by another narrow hallway. But as I stood in the doorway and saw the aquatic prints on the walls within, I knew I was finally in the right place.

Waldman couldn't have planned it better: I'm there to ask him how segmented waterways, mixed signals, and unexpected route changes are confusing to fish. Stream connectivity is vital for resident species that need to make seasonal adjustments, he explains. "Maybe they need to move upstream in the summer to get cooler water, while they might be happier downstream in the winter where there's this less powerful flow and where they don't have to burn as much energy to be there. They need to make seasonal adjustments which are cut off by these dams." But diadromous fish that rely on both fresh and saltwater habitats are the real poster children for that connectivity. In quieting the current and thus disrupting the hydrological signals needed for their upstream passage, impoundments confuse migrating fish. Think of each stretch between two dams as an island, he suggests; when organisms are trapped between dams, there is a loss of genetic diversity. "And the smaller the island, the more island-sized you make a system, the greater chance you have of extirpations of populations between dams. With a small island in the open ocean with ten individuals, there's a greater chance of extinction than with a larger island with a thousand individuals. So you're creating these small subpopulations that may blank out because of that aspect." And as such, their isolation can prevent them from surviving stresses of sediment traps, predation, and increased water temperatures.[8]

Fragmented fish passage, along with the degraded condition of Furnace Pond, its stratification, and accumulation of sediment are all subjects that come up on a walk I take around it with George Jackman early in the summer of 2021. Jackman is an aquatic ecologist, and his professional title is senior habitat restoration manager at the Hudson River nonprofit organization Riverkeeper. The way he puts it, the job is simply to advocate for the rights of rivers, of water, of trees, of the earth itself. He is unlikely to return phone calls and emails and would be the first to tell you his constituents are the fish. Jackman grew up on the South Shore of Long Island, finding in the lagoons of the Great South Bay respite from a difficult and dysfunctional family life. He also happens to be a retired New York Police Department (NYPD) lieutenant, an unexpectedly appropriate background for his current occupation as czar of dam removal in the Hudson Valley. As he puts it, twenty years of experience with "man's inhumanity to man" was valuable training ground for human abuse towards the environment. After leaving the police department, he got a bachelor's degree in biology at Queens College (as a student of John Waldman, I learn later), followed by a doctorate in ecology, education, and behavior at City University of New York Graduate Center.

"Where did our rights come from?" Jackman asks as we begin our walk. Pleased to address the question himself, he says, "They came late to women, late to Native Americans. Bolivia is a country that recognizes the rights of nature," and he cites that nation's legislation which, after generations of mineral mining that ravaged the land, recognizes such rights as that to "pure water and air," "to continue vital cycles," and "to not be affected by mega-infrastructures and development projects that affect the balance of ecosystems and the local inhabited communities." Ecuador, I know, has similar legislation, with a constitution that mandates nature "has the rights to integral respect for its existence and for the maintenance and regeneration of its life cycles, structure, and evolutionary processes." Likewise, rivers in New Zealand have been granted the rights of personhood. "If a corporation can be granted personhood," Jackman asks, "why not a river? Surely bodies of water have more life in them."

As we walk, Jackman automatically catalogues the nonnative species proliferating around us. He vigorously swats a stem of jewelweed as he itemizes the intruders strangling native plants: multiflora, porcelain berry, hemlock wooly adelgid, barberry, and the festive vines of bittersweet ringing the trees. That list is only a prologue to his even more dire assessment of the pond. Turning to the water, he states, "All lakes are born to die," and compares the pond, with its unnatural nutrient load and stratification, to a cancer patient. "Furnace Pond is in senescence," he tells me.

Jackman's tone may seem hyperbolic, but it speaks to the extremes of the circumstances. In December 2023 the International Union for

Conservation of Nature at the United Nations climate summit in Dubai, United Arab Emirates, announced its findings on biodiversity loss: a quarter of the world's freshwater fish are at risk of extinction. The greatest threat is pollution from the fertilizers and pesticides used in farming, sediment congesting the current, and industrial waste and human sewage. Dams and water extraction came in second, and overfishing, invasive species, and disease rounded out the list of hazards.[9] It is not just habitats but migration paths of both water and land species that are suffering. Changing temperatures, habitat fragmentation, roads, and dammed waterways disrupt not only animal habitats but their travel patterns as well. It's not just where they live, it's how they move.[10] All of which is to say, it is not simply individual species at risk but greater avenues of existence, broader systems, and processes long entrenched in the history of place.[11]

On this particular morning, Jackman finds the condition of Furnace Dam revolting and is incredulous when I tell him its hazard class has been reduced from "intermediate" to "low." Federal guidelines use a three-level system to classify dams as low-, intermediate- or high-hazard, categories that are not based on the condition or structural integrity of the dam, or with its capacity to impound water, but rather on the impact downstream should it fail. A Class A, or low-hazard dam, is defined as being unlikely to result in loss of life, with only minor increases to existing flood levels at roads and buildings, while an intermediate hazard, or Class B, dam would result in property damage to isolated homes, flooding of minor roadways, disruption of utilities, possible personal injury, but limited loss of life. With the change in classification, the town board seems inclined to keep the dam stable; repairs and maintenance could run to $750,000, yet in a board meeting in 2020 the general consensus is to keep the pond—referred to as "one of the town's treasures"—intact at least until there is a clear mandate to do otherwise.

The strategy is an unequivocal failure in Jackman's view. As we stand twenty feet downstream from its base, he points out that the sluice, the iron channel built over a century and a half ago to direct the dam's water flow, is corroded, and that water is streaming through the dolomite around the dam. "This is all eroding," he says. "And there is no way to release the pressure on the dam. The water is probably flowing over the dam at about fifty miles an hour. Who knows where it will go [if breached]. It could be catastrophic. Water is leaking through the mortar as well, and it's only going to get worse every winter when it freezes and refreezes, opening up the cracks more and more." Dam removal would reconnect the stream with its floodplain, replenish shoreline habitats, recharge aquifers, repair fish migration routes, and restore the flow of sediments and nutrients.

Remnants of the old iron smelting furnace, the lime quarry, and sections of the lime kiln remain threaded through the woods downstream—as well as the sluice pipe, old stone retaining walls, crumbling foundations, a deteriorating rectangular concrete basin, and a haphazard tumble of cement blocks encrusted with moss attest to the previous era of industry. And if these artifacts are hard to read, so too is the landscape itself. A rock wall to the west just below the dam invites conjecture: was it carved out to make a space in which to store coal or was it formed naturally by the rush of water in the original stream bed? If it's difficult to imagine lives before our own, it is just as hard to explain the contours of the landscape.

It's impossible—for me, anyway—to make sense of these early clues, and the original function in the traces of the old furnace remain just as inscrutable. Still, some part of me appreciates their quiet reference to the history of the place. I know that both here and elsewhere in the Northeast, such archeological relics are read as treasured vestiges of early American enterprise. Especially at this moment, as our culture at large seems to be racing forward at an accelerated speed, efforts to honor local history and the craft found in its handwork and carefully shaped materials are not to be dismissed lightly. Removing the stone walls and foundations is a way of erasing the past, the argument goes. But such questions also signal the inevitable contest between historic preservation and environmental conservation, alternating urgencies in how we define a sense of place. If it is an innate human impulse to try to hang on to bits of the past, we rarely agree on which bits. Is heritage a matter of human ingenuity and industry? Or of thriving woodlands and clean water? Do we want to protect buildings and artifacts or natural systems and resources?

Jackman rejects the battle between the preservation of artifacts and the restoration of ecological balance. The notion that such industrial ruins have value that speaks to our history elicits a snort from him, along with the suggestion that such cheesy nostalgia has about as much worth as the rocks in the old slag heap only feet away. "The town only cares about sentiment," he says. "Dominion over nature is our history. History? What is history? Ask the Native Americans about 'historical dams.'" There is an improvisational debris dam at the small stone footbridge below the dam, and downstream the streambed has been scoured, its banks eroding. "This whole thing should be blown up," he says in disgust. "People talk about controlling the river. I call it enslaving the river."

His disdain calls to mind those ways in which our associations with both landscape and the built world can evolve over time and across different interest groups. The cultural significance of an old stone foundation—or a pond or dam—is not static. Different communities experience these things differently, and in the same way our loyalties and affections about anything else can change, our ideas about economic value or beauty or efficiency are all subject to revision. A community opposed to building a dam may contest its removal within a generation or two. Likewise, concerns for human safety may override nostalgic attachments to a dam and the pond it creates; our cultural preferences are no less volatile than changing climate conditions.[12] That said, Jackman is not sanguine about town legislators acknowledging the ecological impairment of the stratified water, the instability of the structure, or the potential for catastrophic damage to downstream land and homes were it to give way. "When I am on the river it is spiritual," he says. "It's not a resource, it's a life source." To cap his thoughts on the inevitability of human delusion, he quotes the final line of *The Great Gatsby* by F. Scott Fitzgerald: "So we beat on, boats against the current, borne back ceaselessly into the past."

Over time I learn that Jackman breaks into the lyric mode when he gets emotional—which is almost always, when it comes to waterways. It is an engaging, unexpected, and generally persuasive habit. He tends to have a tall walking stick with him on our outings. Along with his oratory, it helps to cast him as a biblical prophet, Isaiah maybe, with his righteous mission, deep fury, dire warnings, and redemptive hope. Yet his genetic make-up also seems to include Edward Abbey's politics and E. O. Wilson's scientific proficiency. It makes sense. His subject of interest is of a scale that can be, perhaps must be, addressed from a variety of viewpoints and perspectives, and I've come to think that a convergence of scientific, literary, and political sensibilities may be required to fully grasp the nature of what is happening here.

And he's right about the degraded condition of the dam. A 2020 engineering assessment cataloged its uncertain structural stability, outlet inoperability, and seepage, along with decrepit masonry and substantial root growth near the abutments, and in the end assigned its condition to some indeterminate zone between "Unsound" and "Unsafe." Evaluated for its capacity to withstand heavy loads of winter ice, floodwater over the spillway itself, and even possible earthquakes, the dam did not meet minimum safety requirements set by NYSDEC. The dam was built on a foundation of limestone and dolomite covered by only a thin veneer of soil, and photographs from the assessment showed bulges in its downstream face; missing masonry and seepage at the toe of the dam; further seepage in the abutment and bank areas; tension cracks and leaks on its downstream face, along with more dislodged masonry; and deteriorating grout at some of the joints in the bedrock. In dry months when little water comes into the pond from the creek, water leaching through fissures in the dam and its surrounding bedrock drains down the pond, with more water going out than coming in. Grout has been applied in the past to patch the downstream face, but those improvised repairs aren't helping much now.

The engineers suggested possible options to bring the dam into compliance with NYSDEC regulations, but these often seemed to be a matter of comparing one unknown with another. Anchors could be installed through the top of the spillway to clamp the dam more securely to be bedrock. Before doing so, however, the material composition of the structure's interior would need to be identified. Concrete? Stone masonry? An aggregate of fieldstone and concrete? Some archaic combination of stone and earthen fill unlikely to have the stability to support interior anchors? All of this is conjecture, though, and boring tests to determine the interior material are necessary before any decision can be made. If such an anchoring system is not feasible, a second option would be to construct a concrete buttress against the downstream face of the dam, in effect building a smaller dam to support the larger, existing dam.

Another option in the report was to lower the height of the dam. With the top two or three feet removed, the structure would be stabilized, though drawing down the impoundment in the process. Replacing the dam was another option. Any new structure, however, would have to conform to current structural and environmental codes, and these are far more stringent and costly than those of the past, making this idea barely feasible. The final option, of course, would be to dismantle the dam altogether. The process would require draining the pond, removing that barrier stone by stone and block by block, returning its channel to a creek, reconfiguring the banks around it with native trees and shrubs, cultivating a wetland, and otherwise revising entirely a centuries-old waterway.

The work would not end there. Removing the dam and its pond would require managing and disposing of the embedded silt. Stratified water and algae blooms are not the only signs that the still water here might also be dead water. Traces of cadmium may linger in the sediment of the pond bed. The chemical element is native to the soil here and is commonly found in the earth's crust, but there is also speculation that its presence is a vestige of the nineteenth-century mining operation on what is now the pond bed. Cadmium can be stirred up in the mining process, its presence increased in the surrounding soil, water, and air. While its origins and current levels remain uncertain, the greater question is what to do about it. Ingesting cadmium can lead to kidney disease, lung damage, and loss in bone density, but even lingering traces in the air can be toxic to humans. If the dam were to be removed and the pond returned to a coursing stream, the contaminant in the sediment would almost certainly be exposed and carried downstream.

Such legacy pollutants figure in to concerns around dam removal. The accumulation of toxic sediment some 120 miles upstream on the Hudson River decades ago provided occasion to reconsider how dams could be removed safely. General Electric plants at Hudson Falls and Fort Edwards had been discharging waste full of polychlorinated biphenyls (PCBs), carcinogens harmful to human health and the environment, into the Hudson River for over forty years, with those toxins settling into the river's sediment in large swaths at the base of the dam. When the Fort Edwards dam was removed in 1973, that sediment was stirred up, its hundreds of tons of contaminated material flowing again into the river, endangering aquatic species and destroying fish habitats. Nine years later, a 200-mile stretch of the river was classified as a federal Superfund site, making it the largest such site in the country.

Decades of controversy ensued. General Electric stalled, questioned the science, and argued to leave the sediments in place in the riverbed to better serve river ecology, but it was ultimately ordered to pay for the clean-up, with specific goals set by the Environmental Protection Agency (EPA). While hotspots remain in the riverbed, protocols defining dredging techniques for the containment and removal of hazardous materials were established that became integral to dam removal.[13] It should be noted, though, that decades after dredging began, these protocols are far from resolved. Although 2015 was the final year of dredging, periodic sampling of sediment since then has consistently found that the goals set by the EPA have not been met. Concentrations of PCBs remain elevated, and after reviewing the most recent data sets in 2023, Tracy Brown, president of Riverkeeper, stated that dredging "for the Upper Hudson has missed the mark in reducing the level of PCBs needed for ecological and human health. It simply wasn't enough. . . . Now is the time for the EPA to reassess what is needed to get the Hudson on a true path to recovery."

But even beyond concerns of toxicity, the sedimentation at Furnace Pond accumulated substantially in the summer of 2019 with the breach of the McKinney Dam just a mile upstream. Silt accumulated from the point of breach all the way down to Furnace Pond. A thin section of the creek half a mile above the pond that had been straightened and channelized back when it was a millstream filled in nearly completely. Immediately after the breach, the water was milky, thick with churned-up soil, and dead fish washed up, including some bass and catfish. As Jake Gosnell, then the park manager, told me, "Whatever wasn't a fish made out pretty well—raccoons, possums, and any animals that feed on dead things."

Gosnell is tuned in to what's happening here. With his baseball cap, ear gauges, bandana, and a respectable amount of ink on his arms, he conveys a hipster vibe, but he's not beyond getting sentimental. In his late thirties now, he grew up in the area and played in the park as a kid, a background that gives him an abiding allegiance to the place. A man of few words, he still becomes animated when he speaks about the stream, the pond, the land around it, shifts in its flow and ecology. "The remnants of Hurricane Ida washed some of the silt downstream, but you can't get rid of all of it," he says, adding that it's still considered a trout stream; too much sediment, though, will shallow the waterway, warming it and rendering it inhospitable to the trout.

Yet leaving the dam in place and the sediment with its presumed contaminants intact has a passive appeal, and not just for reasons of cost, convenience, and corporate liability. We humans are often inclined to allow the turmoils of history to lie undisturbed. Stirring up the grit of the past is rarely appealing, and putting aside those things we are reluctant to address is a time-honored human tradition. Which leaves one to wonder whether prosaic questions of sediment management reflect more entrenched attitudes we have about confronting histories, individual or collective. That said, ecologists increasingly accept the fact the sedimentation is never pristine; and that pollutants—including heavy metals, pesticides, and polycyclic aromatic hydrocarbons (PAHs), a class of chemicals found in coal, crude oil and gasoline—are indisputably embedded in our past.[14] They are in the water and in the ground because we have put them there, and leaving a barrier in place to keep contaminants in place simply piles one ecological error atop the other. Without any decisive approach on how to manage contaminated sediment, it remains a question best addressed for now on a site-to-site basis.

Even six years after the dam breach upstream, much of the sediment remains in a gorge carved in the rock just above Furnace Pond, with the south end of the gorge resembling a small delta. Beyond that, the channel snakes a bit, forming a natural choke point where the banks narrow. Shallow to begin with, it is now more so, and water birds such as egrets are sometimes found foraging there. The Fishkill Creek may be a designated trout stream, but the cool deep springs that qualify it as such are filling in. While temperatures upstream have allowed for a population of native brook trout, the pond itself is stocked annually for brown trout, relying on an $800 annual budget for some 300 fish a year. "It's partly for recreation, the kids who like to fish there," says Gosnell, "but it's also to help keep the ecology in place. Stocking the stream with brown trout just helps to keep it going." While more grasses and shrubs grow along the shore of the pond, forming new shoreline habitats and helping to hold the banks in place, a cool, deep pond just downstream of the breach has vanished completely.

The breach was pretty awful at first, Gosnell says, but it's the way of nature, and the way things—sometimes—take care of themselves. Sediment transport invariably alters what lies in its path, but when allowed to flow rather than settle and collect, it will redistribute itself, find its way, most of it washing down to the mouth. Erosion is the constant, inevitable, and natural state of the earth around us, and it is in the character of the flowing current to drain debris, to redistribute silt and sediment. Which is to say, preventing sediment from downstream flow is rarely justification for keeping a barrier in place. More than once I've heard aquatic ecologists quote the words of hydrologist Luna Leopold: "Rivers are the gutters down which flow the ruins of continents." The reference may be to sediment transport, yet the words resonate with broader meaning about the work of rivers.

John Welsh, a town councilman and longtime local resident, recognizes the complexities of the site. He recalls riding his bike to the pond as a kid and swimming out to a small island at its center. The pond hadn't silted in yet and was a bucolic swimming hole; along with the dam, it was a favorite gathering place for kids. In his seventies now, Welsh has served multiple terms on the town board and is currently the deputy town supervisor. Over the years, he has also served on the volunteer ambulance corps, local cemetery committee, and volunteer fire department. With sandy hair that's gone to gray and an overriding sense of equanimity, he is driven by civic concerns and is one of those community members respected by residents of diverse political convictions and affiliations; whether he is helping a grieving parent find a burial site in the cemetery after the sudden death of a child or explaining the minutiae of town code, he exudes a steadfast dependability. Much of that has to do with his allegiance to the place, his hopes to conserve the natural beauty of the landscape, and his interest in historic preservation.

He's a pragmatist as well, attuned to questions of liability, maintenance costs, structural stability, riparian habitat, public sentiment, and the content and condition of 150 years' worth of sediment. Like many others in the town, he'd like to see the dam maintained and the pond preserved—but only if it makes sense. And he knows that given the dam's identified deficiencies, the "Do Nothing" approach is, as the engineers themselves have stated, "the least acceptable option." Welsh is a neighbor and talking it over with me one morning at my kitchen table, he tells me that the survey of town residents indicated that two thirds of them hope to keep the pond in place. "It's the setting," he says, "the natural beauty of the place." (The survey had a 36.5% response rate, with 74.7% advocating for dam restoration, 12.65% for its dismantling, and 12.65% in want of more information.)

While clarifying the options the town has—shorten the dam's height, reinforce the spillway, replace the dam, remove the dam—NYSDEC does not advocate for any single course of action. Although there may be interest in removing dams for ecological reasons, public safety of a given site rather than environmental stewardship is the agency's focus; its classification system is, as described earlier, based on public safety. Here, rather than dictating replacement, repair, or removal, the agency has left the choice to the town.

Warren Shaw is an engineer in the Division of Water, Bureau of Flood Protection and Dam Safety with NYSDEC in Albany. When I reach him on the phone, he tells me he knows the site and that "Nothing in recent reports has indicated any substantial change in the condition of the dam." But, he adds, past results don't guarantee future results. It doesn't work that way. These dams were built according to standards that are now antiquated. A maintenance plan was put into place that included quarterly reports having mostly to do with visible seepage and overgrowth. And for those twenty-plus years, the town has chosen to leave the dam in place.

By mid-August 2021 the spillway is dry. The state of disrepair in the mechanics of the dam have long prevented any controlled release of water. The maintenance crew at the park had pumped water from the pond the previous summer at considerable cost, between $10,000 to $12,000, to allow the engineering team to do its full evaluation, but the boring tests have yet to be done. This summer, I know the engineers are waiting for dry conditions to test the interior construction of the dam; if it is some improvisational combination of stones and earthen fill packed between the interior and exterior walls, seepage would have long since moistened that earth, making the dam even more unstable.

But waiting for dry conditions in one of the wettest summers in recent history was a fool's errand. Only days later, the remnants of Hurricane

Henri sweep up the East Coast, bringing hard rains and winds inland. In early September, Hurricane Ida, catastrophic for New Orleans, has dire consequences for the Northeast as well. Torrential rains bring over six inches in a day to our county, and overnight, the rain pounds our roof, causing drips from the ceiling. When I walk to the pond the following morning, I slosh through ankle-deep water pooled on the grass on the way to the first cement bridge—which just remains passable. The pathway beyond, put in place decades ago, is in the stream's floodplain. Two small footbridges have disappeared, and it's impossible to say whether they have been inundated or washed away completely. The meadows around them have become a shallow, muddy lake. Whitewater surging through the gorge is rushing fast, down and over the banks of the stream by the park's playgrounds.

Furnace Pond itself is a turgid, muddy slab, flowing slowly and relentlessly towards the dam. A roiling, liquid wall of water pours over the spillway, and I am reminded that 150 years of silt has been accruing here. I'm accustomed to thinking of moving water and still water as two contrasting natural phenomenon that speak to conditions of the human psyche. Looking at the thick blanket of brown sludge surging over the dam now, though, I realize that moving water, or moving water such as this anyway, can convey not just movement and momentum but power of a different order, a brute strength and force capable of sweeping away whatever is in its path. I am reminded of Jackman's comments on our walk earlier in the summer: "Hydropower is the most dangerous power on earth now. And I am attracted to the sound of water. Water and its organisms belong to the people in the state of New York," he had said, and then pointing to the water: "This is my boss."

Remnants of two hurricanes have made it up the East Coast in the course of ten days, and it's been the wettest summer on record. I know this is the new normal, just as I know these antique dams were not designed or built to withstand such flows. In its classification of streams, the US Forest Service designates those that hold water throughout the year as perennial. Intermittent streams are those that hold water during wet portions of the year. Ephemeral channels flow only after rainfall or snowmelt and can sometimes only be identified by exposure of soil or change in leaf litter. Looking at the roiling water around me now, I wonder at our efforts to catalog the different orders of water flow. Only a week or so earlier, the pond had been still, the spillway dry. Immobility and Energy. Nothing changes; everything changes. How strange it is that these two opposing circumstances are the desired ideals between which we so often alternate.

The weather in the Northeast the following summer of 2022 is just as extreme, though this time we face heat and lack of rain. The pond, like so many other waterways across the country, has been stressed over time by both extreme drought and flooding. Jackman is in the area for other work that September, and we decide to take look at Furnace Pond. The stream is a cloudy jade green, and when we get to the pond, we find a proliferation of chartreuse algae blooms streaked with sludge. It's become an incubator for the blooms, and the approximately fifteen feet of sediment that has collected below the spillway is a stew of green muck. The fissures in the dam are dry now, exposing where the leaks are. "Repulsive," Jackman mutters. "I've been a detective and investigator all my life, and this is a sin against nature. The town has no right to do this to the water. This is a crime. It's disgusting. The blooms could kill any dog that drinks from it." Dead water may be a scientific phenomenon defined by a reduced level of oxygen, but it has a corollary in the imagination, and Jackman's disgust could have been channeling Gaston Bachelard's dire speculation on stagnant, sitting water, in which he notes the pool as a symbol of complete and final slumber: "to fulfill an essential psychological function: to absorb shadows, to offer a daily tomb to everything that dies within us each day. Thus, water is an invitation to die."[15]

Highly eutrophic, the condition of the pond is likely not just a result of the drought but of a nutrient load upstream. Eutrophication occurs when an overload—usually caused by human activity—introduces excessive natural elements such as phosphorus and nitrogen into a body of water. The process feeds algae growth, reduces oxygen, disrupts the balance in the aquatic ecosystem, and degrades water quality. This section of the creek is only a couple of miles south of its source, limiting the number of possible upstream causes for the excessive nutrients: a hunting club breeds pheasants and ducks, and the pollutants downstream could be a product of their excrement. Or the source could be agricultural fertilizers from a small family farm just upstream draining into the watershed. Both might be to blame. Until there is a coordinated effort for water testing between the town and landowners, the source of the pollutants remains unidentified.

Jackman and I walk the path back up the creek to the park entrance. An egret stands motionless at the far edge of the pond. A spiky purple wildflower in the polygonum family, a native perennial that grows in swampy areas, is blossoming on a small island in the pond. It is tempting on this late summer day to bask in these incidental moments of natural beauty. But a number of ash trees, afflicted with emerald ash borer, have been taken down; the invasive pests that feed on their bark and leaves have left them weakened and diseased. Hemlocks are withering from an infestation of woolly adelgid that munch on the tree's starches and disrupt the flow of nutrients to its needles. The area is under duress, the forest as stressed as the pond and stream. In the coming week, though, residents will be celebrating OctoberFest, an autumn holiday. The lawns are being mowed, game courts set up, and tents erected for community members to come to the park for activities that include the chicken dance, barrel racing, and stein hoisting. It is impossible not to reflect on what we are paying attention to, impossible not to note the disconnect between the fastidious care bestowed on the cultivated lawns and the installation of beer tents and the putrid water and disease-ridden forest around it.

The park suddenly seems to be Exhibit A of how we choose to care for the landscape, with festive entertainment often trumping the stewardship of natural systems. If the park is a community asset, it begs the question of what is meant by *community*; and whether it is simply a human collective or one that includes other species, animal and plant alike. As a public park, it is a restorative place—but part of that today may have to do with restoring a sense of responsibility, recognizing what belongs here and what doesn't, and acknowledging what is sometimes called interspecies empathy.

The following winter is one of the warmest on record. A February morning is sunny, the temperature in the mid-fifties. Water is pouring through the cracks and fissures of rock on the eastern side of the dam at almost double the rate it did a year ago. The roots of trees growing around the dam continue to break up the soil and rock, allowing ever more water to stream through. As the engineers predicted two years earlier, the seepage has only increased with time. I know that another option for this site is benign neglect, simply allowing the dam to fail on its own—letting the leaks grow, continuing to watch the water find its own improvisational paths among the stones and through the embankments. Eventually, such substantial leakage would allow for the water on either side of the dam to equalize, thus lessening the weight of water against the stone. It would certainly be easier to remove the upper levels of the structure with the water level so diminished. Some of these antique dams were built with massive keystones in their foundation, stones that could be dislodged and removed to lower the water level quickly if necessary. But as with so many relic structures, there are no plans to reference, no way of knowing the original design and structure of the foundation. And hoping that negligence will produce desired results in a timely and productive manner is always a risky proposition.

The equipment needed to conduct the boring test is difficult to schedule, and the drought and subsequent low water of the previous summer had been a missed opportunity. The idea that the tests could be conducted in May is floated, but the option is rejected, as spring run-off has raised the water level. Testing is scheduled instead for August 2023. It could happen. By June, the pond is only two or three feet deep, stagnant, streaked and marbled with algae blooms. Several weeks without rain have lowered the level of the water a couple of feet below the spillway, and more water is surging through leaks on the east side of the dam. But then weeks of rain follow, and by August, water is again pouring steadily over the dam and down around the abutment and bedrock on the east side. Once again, there is far too much water, and plans for testing are scrapped. Another summer has passed, and I am reminded again of the hubris in imagining that the tests can be run on schedules that conform to human convenience.

Things can come apart in different ways. A management plan for the Fishkill Creek watershed drafted in 2005 had outlined a multidimensional approach for dam removal that took in longitudinal factors both upstream and down, including fish passage, sediment flow, and the flow rate of water; lateral factors linked riparian health, changes in stream width, species habitat, and groundwater tables. The plan also considered vertical interactions that ranged from the water column to canopy cover, along with temporal interactions such as the condition of the stream over time, its meander, its biotic composition, and changes in species habitat. It was a comprehensive plan, but that was all more than twenty years ago, and Jake Gosnell anticipates that the dam's future will be determined in a more extemporaneous manner when it breaches. "There'll be a lot of upset, and the community will be asked for input. Then there'll be a lot of 'Oh, I fished there or ice skated there when I was a child.' But not all that many people really use it today. That fact will come out. Which is not the best circumstance under which to make a sound decision." He is frustrated. The monthly town board meeting is held the following night, and when I check the agenda, I see nothing about the dam has been scheduled.

Years go by without resolution. Dam removal can be a matter of ecological urgency, human safety, land use, and financial concern, all of which makes it a hot button political issue. Public scrutiny doesn't necessarily advance the cause, and Fran Dunwell has told me that local legislators can win or lose elections based on how these decisions are made and perceived. By now I know that even the most casual estimates put the cost of dismantling the dam at well over a million dollars. Yet I suspect it's not just the high price tag that is stalling any action to disassemble the deteriorating structure. Spending money to get rid of things often rubs against the municipal ethic. People would generally rather build things.

But there is another way to consider costs. Economic arguments used to favor dam construction may cite hydroelectric power, irrigation, recreation, flood control, water supply, navigation, or some other human use, all of which can be quantified in cost-benefit analyses. The fiscal equations are more obscure when calculating the costs of losing a free-flowing river: displaced homes and communities, flooded sites, vanishing wetlands, loss of aquatic habitat, and species extinction.[16] Environmental economics is a nascent field of study in 2024, with some financial institutions, philanthropists, and ecologists looking for ways to assign market value to preserving nature. Such efforts might include preserving farmland instead of developing it, valuing woodlands and forests for carbon sequestration, and removing obsolete dams. Such "ecosystem services" are not without controversy: Conservatives will find fault with such protections and the regulation they come with, while progressives are skeptical about viewing the natural world as a commodity to be monetized.[17]

That said, there may be reasons to consider economic value as an incentive for restoring ecological health. The measurements we use in quantifying what we value can be elusive. The American chestnut trees once integral to these woodlands are long gone. Infestations of spongy moths have degraded the oak trees. The hemlock and ash trees are threatened as well. It is a cliché to point out that the natural world is in a state of constant change, but those changes are coming faster and more frequently now. I think of the piles of turquoise, amber, lavender slag shining under the moldy leaves in the woods near the pond, mementoes of an earlier industrial era and reminders of how quickly those things we cherish can lose their meaning and worth.

2023 ends without a path forward. Although the dam and its fissures and leaks are recognized as urgent concerns, the unpredictable rhythms of drought and deluge have made it difficult to schedule the boring tests. It's been over two decades since a master plan for the park recommended that the dam be removed. Maintenance costs during that time have covered trail and tree work near the dam, an engineer's report, thousands spent on pumping pond water out for a test that never happened, and installing—and occasionally repairing—a chain link fence around the structure. "We have to make a decision," the town supervisor says: reconstruct the dam or bring it down and landscape the wetland that remains. But a new administration will take charge in 2024, and what happens next is anyone's guess.

If ambiguities persist around the future of the dam and the pond, new notions of community can still transpire from time to time. On a cloudy March morning in 2024, I meet David Rothenberg at the park. He is a jazz musician, composer, and professor of Philosophy and Music at the New Jersey Institute of Technology. Driven by a respect for the mysteries of bioacoustics and an abiding commitment to ecology, he has recorded—and played music with—a wide variety of performers in his interspecies symphonies. Over the years, his musicians have included humpback whales, katydids and crickets, blue jays, mockingbirds, and nightingales. On this particular morning, though, the pond is high, and it's the aquatic plants and insects he'll be accompanying.

In his recently published *Secret Sounds of Ponds*, Rothenberg writes "You begin to become excited by a tiny, unexpected event. It could be the bubbles and movement of plant oxygen or the sound of photosynthesis or an unknown creature, something you cannot see, never see what you hear, his identity, her identity, mixing in with the rhythms that make you feel enlightened, alive, electrically charged all over." When I learn that he lives in a neighboring town, I am quick to send him an email suggesting an outing to Furnace Pond. He responds just as quickly.

"A good pond for a concert," Rothenberg says when we meet there. In his sixties, he has the quiet manner of someone who has long understood how to defer to the unknown, and collaboration seems to come to him intuitively. He takes in the weeds, the leaves, all the drowning detritus just barely visible in the cloudy water. The shallow edge of the pond, or the littoral zone, is an active transitional area where sunlight reaches the bed, where weeds grow, and where there is a diversity of plant life, food, and habitat for fish, invertebrates, reptiles, and shorebirds. Or as Rothenberg says, "It has a mushy bottom. That's where stuff happens."

He's not the only one to think so. Freshwater soundscapes, for all their lyrical possibilities, also offer solid data. Camille Desjonquères uses bioacoustics and biogeography in researching climate change, and she cites the pioneering integration of these two disciplines in forecasting "shifts in breeding phenology, geographic distribution and species persistence."[18] Of the information embedded in the bottom of a pond, she explains that "All these rhythms and even the faint squeals are likely to be bubbles in a pond very rich in organic matter, a lot of vegetation. The sediment is very muddy, so we hear photosynthesis, decomposition, and the respiration of plants themselves, often more rhythmic and musical sounding than the underwater creatures. Whenever there is a flow of energy in the plant that is continuous and regular, we hear rhythmic sounds."[19]

Passive Acoustic Monitoring is an emerging tool offering scientists opportunities to use soundscapes—biological, geophysical, and anthropogenic—in their research. Rothenberg has also been accompanied on his outings by Ben Gottesman, a member of the K. Lisa Yang Center for Conservation Bioacoustics at Cornell University and professor in the Natural Resources Department at Cornell. Gottesman explores the role bioacoustics can play in furthering conservation and habitat management. Finding that aquatic soundscapes offer valuable data on ecological dynamics, he has written that "Biological sound sources represent a subset of the biological community present. By quantifying the diversity and occurrences of biological sounds, it is possible to assess animal activity patterns and in some cases evaluate biodiversity or habitat condition."[20]

Now Rothenberg takes out a hydrophone, essentially a waterproof microphone, attaches a ten-meter-long cord to it, then tosses it about ten feet out into the pond. He plugs the other end of the cord into a Sony field audio recorder and sets up the speaker. And then we listen. A little clicking. Some scratching, whispers. *Dut, dut, dut.* Then a dripping, fluid and dissonant, and possibly a bubble. But it is a different alphabet of sound that can't be replicated with the letters I use, nor is my ear accustomed to these soft acoustic rhythms and patterns. Still, the sounds confer a different kind of intimacy with this place I thought I knew so well.

I can just barely discern the remote muffled popping of plants photosynthesizing, releasing tiny bubbles of oxygen in the process, then a delicate rhythmic scratching. A water boatman, Rothenberg says, a little streamlined water bug named for its oarlike legs. When I look it up later, I read that it is the loudest animal on earth relative to body size. I learn also that it is known for its singing penis.

It's not like beluga whales, Rothenberg says of these soft bioacoustics. "Ponds have always been *right here!* It fascinates me that we know so little about them. Scientists have been recording these sounds for months, for years. There is a lot of data. Memory and storage are cheap. But none of it is understood yet." He tells me that ecologists listening to these concerts can identify only about ten percent of the sounds and often disagree on whether the musician is a plant or a bug. Yet if the subtle murmurs coming from a pond on an early spring morning might not hold up in a legal dispute over the rights of rivers and streams, mountains, forests, and rock formations, their quiet adamance makes an argument that seems persuasive in some broader judicial system.

The unknown character of Rothenberg's accompanists doesn't seem to disappoint him much. I am accustomed to thinking—now, in this time, in this world—that we are after more knowledge, more information. Generally speaking, that may be true. But listening now at the edge of the pond, I find myself encountering new levels of mystery. A slight gust blows over the water, and a crow shrieks in the distance. Rothenberg joins in the ensemble then, adding a layer of electronic sound with his iPad synthesizer, joining in with the aquatic plants and bugs. The sounds evoke wind instruments, a keyboard, a tapping and strumming, a steady techno beat, and other, more indeterminate sounds. Waves and pitches vary. Minutes later, he takes out his clarinet and its soulful notes bring a new dimension to the improvised concert. For a moment or two there is a plaintive duet with the geese at the far end of the pond. Rothenburg doesn't do much to his sound files. He might change the speed, the pitch, the level of resonance, the dial between dry and effected sound. "With these simple tools," he says, "I inhabit the sonic world of the pond."

With Rothenberg on the clarinet, the fusion of the electronic notes, the little water boatman beneath the surface, a weed absorbing light, the crows calling overhead, the wind and the water lapping at the bank, it all makes for an idea of community different in spirit from the gatherings that occur more regularly here. Other systems, other species, other frequencies—but we're all here. The small orchestra of ordinary sounds, some known, others remote and enigmatic, captures something of the interstitial moment on this cusp between winter and spring. It's a fitting soundtrack for all the uncertainties visited upon this site. What remains certain, though, is the inclusive character of our little assembly, transient and convened for only a few minutes on a breezy March morning. It may not be exactly what you would call interspecies empathy, but it seems like a good start.

There's a little splash from the pond mic. Then a soft pop. A common backswimmer, maybe. "Interesting things always happen," Rothenberg says. "They can hear us too."

Figure 3. McKinney Pond has become a floodplain braided with native grasses and shrubs.

After the Breach

McKinney Dam

Every dam should have an existential crisis.

—John Waldman[1]

When the McKinney Dam just upstream from Furnace Pond failed in the summer of 2019, it was what is known as "a sunny day breach," an ominous but accurate term for a failure that occurs gradually and for no sudden reason: no heavy rainfall, no catastrophic flood, no ice floes, no clogged spillway or artificial channeling. Technically, it's a failure that occurs under normal operating conditions, the ordinary failure of so many human endeavors that are just a matter of time, of ordinary attrition, disregard, and neglect. Here, it followed a timeline common to calamity: The damage to both the dam and the waterway was decades in coming, then instantaneous. Time passes, there's a bit of slippage, sediment rearranges itself, a stone tumbles out of place and then some structural component is gone, leading to catastrophic failure. It was, in fact, a sunny May afternoon when I drove by what I had known to be a serene pond for thirty years and saw it was now a barren mudflat.

The dam, fifteen feet high and eighty-four feet long, had been built by hand in 1915 with local stone and masonry. Local historians speculate that it replaced an earlier, more rudimentary barrier, likely for a grist mill built in the early nineteenth century. Maps and documents of the area record saw, woolen, and grist mills established in the late 1700s at this juncture of the creek. With a general store and post office, the early settlement known as Crouse's Store served workers in the numerous iron ore mines in the area, who used the lumber, textiles, and flour provided by the mills. Old photographs of the gristmill, standing until the 1950s, show a barn with clapboard siding, a gambrel roof, and the spare elegance one often finds in such rural buildings. Now, only its old stone foundation remains.

It was not uncommon along these tributaries for an early mill dam to be upgraded or replaced entirely with a more substantial hydroelectric dam in the early twentieth century. The first modern water turbine had been developed in the mid-nineteenth century, and soon after it became the fashion in country house design to install hydroelectric power. The dam at McKinney Pond was a run-of-river dam, its flow above and below the dam roughly equal. Its impoundment was not intended to serve as a reservoir but rather to harness water from Fishkill Creek to generate hydroelectric power for the estate of Glenn Ford McKinney and his wife, Jean Webster, author of the 1912 epistolary novel *Daddy-Long-Legs*. Their elegant nineteenth-century Georgian house was surrounded by spacious formal gardens, and it only made sense that they would want to replace gaslight and candles with incandescent light in the style of the day.

In more recent years, the pond created by the dam was flanked on one side by a forest of white pine and Norway spruce planted generations ago, and on the other side by a small family farm. Sediment amassing in the pond over the last century had accumulated in a kind of wedge shape against the dam, working as a makeshift sealant to any gaps in the structure. Over time, though, the finer soil collecting at the base of the dam had begun to seep beneath its foundation, eventually allowing coarser sediment to flow through as well. Ultimately, the seepage became such that the volume and pressure of water pushed the sediment through the dam's foundation, by now somewhat degraded. Hydraulic pressure, acting as a siphon, sucked out water, mud, and silt, and the millpond drained in a single day. Within hours, what had been a tranquil, stream-fed, ten-acre pond became a muddy flat with a thin creek winding through it.

Engineers evaluating the breach days later had used a thirty-foot-long steel probe to measure the area under the structure from the upstream to downstream sides and found a scour as much as nine feet below what was thought to be the bottom of the dam. Sediment left behind by the breach made it difficult to assess the downstream side of the dam more precisely, but it was enough to conclude that its structural integrity was at risk. That said, the sixty-foot spillway remained intact, and the fact that the dam was no longer capable of impounding water was clear only when one looked closely at the flow coursing through its base on the downstream side. A minor turbulence, only a slight roiling area on the surface of the water, and a nearby sweep of sediment are slim but sufficient evidence of the current streaming through the baseline leak.

The creek was quick to carve its channel through the silt and mud left behind by the pond and took only weeks to revert to its original grade and to its earlier bed of sand, pebbles, and cobble. But the mudflat itself was saturated with water; when I tried to step onto its surface a few weeks after the breach, my boot sank ten inches into ooze. Much of the water was still there. It had just rearranged itself, below the ground now instead of above it, creating a wetland that was something like a vast ten-acre sponge. I stepped back quickly. The break in the dam remained out of view with the creek far below the level of the spillway on both sides of the barrier and no discernible difference between the water level of the creek upstream and downstream. But such an interplay between the seen and unseen is often the case with damage.

The mudflat, it turns out, served as an incidental seedbank, largely for native species. Sprouts of new growth meadowed in a matter of weeks to native grasses, mostly sawgrass, a leafy green sedge that grows in wetlands. Purple loosestrife appeared on the banks as well, along with barberry and knotweed, all nonnative species. And the Fishkill Creek had resumed a steady flow, only a couple of miles south of its source at Pray Pond where a number of thin streams converge at the base of Clove Mountain. At the turn of the last century, a local inventor had designed, patented, and manufactured a plow to mark, score, cut, and otherwise harvest ice from Pray Pond for refrigeration. With that enterprise long abandoned, the pond is known more now for being the source of the creek, and today it is wide, shallow, covered with beds of water lilies, silted in at some areas and marshy, thick with willows where the various mountain streams seep into it.

Yet the creek's actual origins are not quite so decisive, lying not only in the streams that converge in Pray Pond but in a spring about three quarters of a mile north. On property owned by a private hunting club, Clove Spring is not easily accessed. On the drizzly June day I finally secure entry, the short walk seems like its own small pilgrimage; that I am searching out a storied water source makes the endeavor feel almost primal. The spring is marked on the earliest maps of the area, and local lore suggests it is the reason early European colonists settled in the valley in the early 1700s. It's easy to believe. The valley sits above an immense aquifer, sand and gravel deposits that can store great quantities of water, and the alluvial soil there is full of nutrients that make it especially fertile. Corn and sorghum used to feed the birds raised by the club flourish in some of the meadows here, while other fields are thick with clover and varieties of wild native grasses, all of it framed by woodlands of maple, hickory, oak. Still misted and dripping with the morning's rainfall, the path to the spring reads as a verdant Arcadian patch, and for a moment I feel as though I may have stepped into some Greek myth.

A small wooden footbridge has been built just over the spring, and upstream the water is placid. But just beneath the bridge, the surface is surging into a small manmade pool. One historical account calls the spring "a fountaining brook," a lyrical description that is also entirely accurate.[2] The spring is a continuous and irresistible birth, wrote Bachelard, and that, too, fits what's happening here. The churning pool scatters the reflection of trees and sky into an effervescent composition of splintered light and water. A glistening rainbow trout nearly a foot and a half long glides into view in the pool, then several others slide in behind it. The water temperature here remains consistently in the mid-fifties throughout the year, and as rainbow trout, a native cold water species, require clear, cool oxygenated water and clear gravel areas for spawning, they serve as indicators of aquatic health.

The spring continues to pour from the earth year-round, by some accounts at several hundred gallons of water per minute, even in droughts. Remnants of a concrete trough built in an earlier effort to channel the pure, clear water remain in the creek bed next to the spring. But it's not just the ceaseless rush of cool water that is so restorative. I find myself surprisingly gratified to learn that waterways can't always claim a precise source or single point of origin, and that sometimes they can begin in sites as varied as a mountain stream and groundwater stored deep in the earth's crust, pressured to seep upwards from its own vast aquifer.

Fishkill Creek's upper stretch qualifies as a headwater stream, a kind of waterway with various definitions. One formal calculation identifies it as a "stream segment in the upper reach of a nontidal stream where the average annual flow of the segment is 5 cubic feet per second or less."[3] Often, though, proximity to source identifies such streams as well, and a less formal definition is that headwaters are simply the smallest, thinnest segment of a river or stream furthest from the point where it terminates. Whatever the terms of definition, such streams in the Northeast are stamped with the character of the woodlands and meadows through which they flow. The leaves, twigs, branches, seeds, and other organic detritus they collect offer habitat for species downstream and are the basis for the aquatic food web. And when those areas are overwhelmed by flood and high waters, such streams can replenish organisms that have been buried or washed away. They also offer habitat for both their own aquatic and terrestrial animals, along with cool, moist corridors for animal passage along the waterway.[4] Put more simply, what happens upstream affects everything that happens downstream—both an ecological principle and reliable metaphor for events and circumstances beyond the watershed.

A failed dam only a couple of miles from the source of the stream may seem to do little to serve fish migration, but I'm reminded of Waldman's explanation that dam removal and aquatic connectivity—wherever it happens—is always restorative. If headwaters provide the building blocks for what happens downstream, open passage upstream can especially benefit resident species needing seasonal adjustment. In addition, if pollutants drain into a free-flowing system, fish are able to find refuge that wouldn't be unavailable if they were confined to a single area. Connectivity, I am reminded again, can begin in unlikely places.

Because the McKinney Dam breached over time, the sediment flushed downstream was not as heavy as it might have been. Silt had also remained embedded in the bed of the drained pond, transforming it into a gigantic earthen sponge. The breach was not catastrophic; the transport of sediment load is what streams *do*. That said, what did wash downstream altered the aquatic habitat and reduced the fish population in Furnace Pond, situated a mile or so south. Even in lesser amounts, such sediments can be damaging to invertebrates and hinder the sight-feeding of some vertebrates; its particles were visible on plant material downstream, visible in the turbidity of the water, visible in reshaping the creek and pond beds downstream. Because Furnace Pond remains dammed, the additional sediment load rendered it more shallow, warmer, and even less hospitable to native aquatic species.

A year later, a few sycamore saplings and some cottonwoods had begun to take root. Sedge, purple verbena, and cut grass had started to grow in as well, though the saplings and shrubs already started to show sign of deer browse. With the new channel well on its way to finding its course, it was not premature to steady the banks with more plantings. With support from Riverkeeper, a squad from the Hudson River Estuary Program planted some 200 seedlings across the floodplain trees, among them red, sugar, and silver maples, river birch, white pine, black willow, pussy willow, and silky dogwood. The planting was part of the agency's Trees for Tribs, a program offered by NYSDEC to help private landowners, nonprofits, and municipalities restore stream buffers; along with providing erosion control, the plantings absorb high water during floods, enhance wildlife habitat, and provide shade to keep water cool.

A forested floodplain also reduces damage from flooding, recharges groundwater, and generally absorbs far more water than a treeless one, while its leaves and debris provide organic matter for the stream ecosystem.[5] The trees and shrubs also stabilize the fine-grade sediment left behind on either side of the channel, shade out invasive plants, and prevent excessive evaporation. The saplings, contained in unsightly olive green polyvinyl tubes meant to protect the new growth from hungry deer, rabbits, and groundhogs, were scattered amid the thicket of scraggly grasses and shrubs. Their bases were protected by squares of synthetic black fabric, the whole arrangement secured by thin wooden pickets and plastic ties.

The pond, once a habitat for beavers, blue herons, mallards, and waterbirds of all sorts, has vanished. With the shining buffet table below no longer available to them for foraging, the bald eagles nesting in the upper reaches of the white pines have moved on elsewhere. The two swans are gone as well. Members of an introduced species that commonly find habitat in fresh water, the pair had nested along the secluded channels of the upper stream for over a decade. The elongated curvature of their slender necks and occasional flutter of wingbeat as they drifted across the pond on a summer day suggested an aristocracy of waterfowl. Some unexpected equation of weight and grace gave them an ornamental poise that seemed a relic from another time. I find myself questioning how to define beauty: is it an arrangement of white feathers, July light, and still water, or is it the promise of an emerging forest?

Eighteen months later, more native rushes and sedge have taken root across the floodplain, as has purple verbena, native and inviting to pollinators. In ecological parlance, the floodplain is becoming a healthy riparian buffer offering a stabilized stream bank, sediment and flood control, and temperature moderations. It supports stream flow, filters runoff water, reduces erosion, and generally improves stream health. Such buffers accommodate a variety of shrubs and trees, a messy understory and overstory, and shade trees that provide ample leaf litter and other woodland debris.[6]

When I go down to take a look and step onto the soggy meadow, a great blue heron lifts from a thicket of grass twenty feet downstream. These wading birds can adapt to all kinds of wetlands, and I wonder if it is a recent arrival or a tenant from the original pond. Its presence likely has to do with the beavers upstream that have been assembling their own dam. The emerging pool behind it and the downed trees around it offer the heron nesting sites. Fast-growing eastern cottonwood saplings that take to the banks of streams and rivers have started to grow in as well. What was once a pond bed is now a scraggly meadow, and even a moderate rain forms thin rivulets. The word *tributary*, derived from the Latin *tributum*, means something contributed or paid, and one definition is a smaller body of water that flows into a larger one. But a common alternative, and the one that seems most fitting this afternoon, is simply a factor that contributes to something that happens.

Stepping across the floodplain now, I find that the sheath of dead grass disguises what is wet and dry ground. The water here has not yet settled into its final route. Barberry with red berries grow on its edges too, and cattails have just started to grow where the ground is especially moist. The thicket of phragmites upstream may flourish too. The bittersweet vine that is roping its way through the branches and girdling the trunks of so many trees near my own house just a mile down the road has not yet made an appearance. It is tempting to speculate that native plants may take root first, even though nonnative species that favor disturbance, roads, and edges of fields may threaten them soon. When they will appear, too, is an unknown.

The impulse to eradicate exotic plants and plant native trees and shrubs seems ironic; for all the logic of removing dams to let the streams and their shores resume their own routes, conventional ideas about letting nature take its course invariably come up against a need for human intervention, and it is difficult to grasp the exact equation of these two practices that will put things to rights. Such is the paradox with which we conduct our relations with the natural world today. "These are high energy systems and environments," Scott Cuppett has told me. "Streams move around. The channel changes. The movement of sediment and water changes over time. Wait it out. Time will tell. We planted very quickly here, but I usually like to wait before planting—see what happens first." Follow the path of the water, I hear him saying, advocating not simply for patience, but for an attentiveness to natural conditions.

He was right. It can take years for sediment to settle. A few weeks later, a December rainstorm caused the creek to flood. High water can be mesmerizing in the way it obscures and alters the familiar, and once it has subsided days later, I see how the downpour has caused the flow of water to realign itself, reconfiguring the contours of the channel. The chaotic current has smashed the grasses flat in this direction and that, and a narrow section of the creek has widened, a bend in it now a bit more of a bend. Elsewhere, thin rivulets draining the adjacent hillside have carved new improvisational paths through the weeds. It's a dynamic system. Some of the tubing securing the saplings has twisted and bowed, pickets have toppled, and the squares of black fabric have been blown and displaced. The whole operation has the look of a gameboard, in which the game, the pieces, indeed the rules of play in their entirety have not only been suddenly interrupted but revised altogether.

In archaic English, the word *slang* referred to a narrow strip of land, sometimes adjacent to a stream or river. It is not necessarily a floodplain but can serve as such, a thin, little stretch of earth that can become liquid. Its meaning and substance can change with conditions, just as a word may change quickly in sense and usage, depending on circumstances. I am taken by this unexpected alignment of language and landscape, finding it a welcome reminder of the changeable nature of what we think of as sure; and how those things we depend on for certainty can become slippery themselves, sliding out of what we think they are and into something else.

Looking at the stream now, I see again how the passage of water and its mutability are such a part of our thinking and our speech. What occurs on the floodplain is hard to predict, and how to manage or intervene in its direction is not necessarily clear beyond a few known facts: don't try to straighten the channel; encourage vegetation to grow; allow for a floodplain. Beyond that, let the water find its way. We talk about *leaving things alone* or about *nature taking its course,* but questions persist about what we can manage and regulate and what is best left to nature, about what is and isn't beyond human control, and about the hubris that allows us to confuse the two.

The river continuum concept considers a river or stream in its longitudinal entirety, following the shifting physical gradients from the narrow riffles and falls of its headwaters to the wider and more quiet areas of its mid-reaches, to the often more turbid sections at its mouth. The stream begins in shaded woodlands that keep the water cool and limit photosynthesis. Its mid-reaches are wider, warmer, and quieter; greater sunlight nurtures greater plant growth, along with the insects that feed on those plants. As the waterway approaches the mouth, there may be fewer rapids, increased turbidity, and quiet backwaters with dense aquatic plants. It is an idea that takes in the shifting systems of the waterway, the biological continuum of water and shoreline, their plant and animal species, understanding all these as a sequence of integrated concerns.[7] While the concept hasn't always seemed like an adequate framework for stream systems—not all of them have shaded headwaters, desert steams may not have a lot of vegetation or leaf litter, and intermittent streams in the arid West may dry up—the idea of viewing a river as an ecological progression from source to mouth holds up.[8]

A fragmented waterway disrupts the continuum. As John Waldman says, "If you then put in a dam midway, and let's say it's the kind of dam where you release the bottom waters from the reservoir, all of a sudden it's warmer on the reservoir surface than it is in the outflow of the dam, and the biota now has to make an accommodation to that. So you may have a warmwater bass fishing reservoir behind the dam, but then you have excellent trout fishing, cold water species below the dam. And there are a lot of rivers around this country where there are excellent renowned fisheries below dams in places you wouldn't expect. But these cold water releases have created these artificial habitats, so that's breaking up the continuum."[9]

What was once McKinney Pond has become its own short stretch of continuum. A corridor of water, it has started to take on a long, gentle S-curve, evidence of the way a stream wants to bend, to slow down, to deviate from following the center of its path. The northern edge of the pond and some five hundred indeterminate feet within the water itself, along with a series of steel pins at a roadside and a concrete right-of-way monument, had long served as a property marker for the landowners on either side. Now that the pond has vanished, that boundary has become indistinct, and the location of the property line remains unresolved. It may be convenient to use bodies of water to demarcate land ownership, but the water demonstrates just as easily how ill-suited it is to the task. In recent years, such questions have come predictably into play across broader landscapes; as ice thaws and glaciers retreat, divides once determined by water drainage are being redefined, in some cases calling national boundaries into question. In 2023, a section of the border between Switzerland and Italy required renegotiation when the flow of Alpine meltwater shifted direction.

The creek itself, indifferent to such artificial boundaries, establishes its own bends. In common usage, a meander implies a kind of purposeless rambling, but in a stream it conforms more strictly to the laws of physics. A result of erosion, the circuitous course of a meander is determined by slope, the volume of flow, velocity, and the material of the bed, whether silt, granite, or cobblestone. The grade of the creek here is slight, and the bed is composed largely of its original sand, pebbles, and cobble; upstream it is mixed, even more coarse. Figuring in as well is shear stress, the force that comes when the different layers of water slide parallel to the surface and against each other, twisting around themselves in a corkscrew motion. But all these factors can change from day to day, week to week, and the process, while continuous, is not consistent.

Yet the creek's bends are also the result of something beyond local conditions: centrifugal force, in which the earth's rotation pushes a moving object outward, propels the faster water to the outside edge of the bend, leaving the water beneath it to spiral, carrying the sediment to the inside of the turn. The surface of the spiraling water moves more quickly than the water near the bed of the stream, slowed by the rocks and gravel in its way and making for a redistribution of sediment that increases over time. Which is to say, streams want to turn. It may just be a little patch of floodplain under a gray winter sky, but there is something reassuring in knowing that this realignment also looks to the great tilt and spin of the earth and that this small stretch of stream conforms to a greater sense of planetary order. When Cuppett said that the stream will find its way, he is referring to both the immediate circumstances of gradient and surface as well as to some larger terrestrial directive.[10]

Small wonder that water often brings the imagination to life; when we speak of consciousness, it is in terms of how it *streams* and how thoughts run in *currents*. *Flow* is the word used to capture the state of being "when consciousness is harmoniously ordered."[11] That May day when the dam breached was also the day a close friend went into surgery for a cancerous tumor, the same day, too, that my husband and I had our first dinner with our son's future mother- and father-in law. Would I remember that these events had occurred on the same day had the ground beneath the dam remained intact? I know that such random adjacent events are meaningless except in the archive of personal memory where a radical rearrangement of water can become associated, in some unfathomable way, with events crucial to one's being; where shifting waters can have some tenuous affiliation with an adjustment in the weights and measures that are central to one's life. And I have found that in the exchanges about rivers, creeks, and their impoundments, we often find ourselves talking about issues and concerns that are braided with human behavior and enterprise.

Perhaps such thoughts are superfluous, simply further evidence that when we look to the exterior world, we are likely to see only ourselves and our own concerns. But it is also possible that when we see these alignments between ourselves and the natural world, we sense that our own human systems can find compatibility with natural ones. Such analogies can connect us to a greater sense of order, and it is only human to go through life looking for them. These commonalities help us decipher experience, understand ourselves and our place in things. When we find such correlations in the natural world—in the way a tributary finds its way to the river, in the way a walking stick insect disguises itself as a branch, in the way a cloud becomes rain—we may find some instruction about forces of certainty and uncertainty and all the other inevitabilities of human experience.

But if it is easy, for me at least, to search for extraneous meaning, to be swept up by the psychological implications here, in the end, of course, it makes more sense to simply return to those considerations belonging to the stream bed, the pond, and the land around it; to quiet my own associations and simply see what is there in the world. These analogies are never as precise as we think, and I know it is a mistake to adhere to them too closely.

The entire question of whether to leave these old dams, obsolete in terms of their original function, in place or to dismantle and remove them speaks to some core of human belief and principle. This part of the Hudson Valley was once a place of industry, pitted with ore beds, and when the beds had been depleted, they were filled with water to make the ponds and impoundments that exist today. I am reminded again that there is something in still water that appeases human agitation, that brings out what is peaceable in ourselves. Seen through the lens of evolutionary psychology, the reflection of light on quiet water has an intuitive appeal. Drinking pools are what saved our ancestors' lives on the savannah,[12] and that same primal brain continues to be transfixed by still water. It's probably why suburban homeowners pour dyes—with names like Crystal Blue, Sapphire, Twilight Blue—into their koi ponds and little lawn pools. We are hardwired to find an equilibrium in the view of still water. Even the word *reservoir* conveys a sense of sufficiency, supply, providence. Its definition in the Oxford English Dictionary carries an ecclesiastical implication as well that reaches to the protection and preservation of the spirit, something that is set apart "to be dealt with by a superior authority." A reservoir may raise water temperature, slow its flow, trap its sediment, and menace aquatic life, yet the word also resonates with reassurance and the idea that there is enough and more to sustain us.

But the high cost of removing a privately owned dam such as this can be prohibitive. These old structures, whether built for sawmills or hydroelectric power, served the economic purposes of a community and were constructed as a public trust, a resource serving the public good. Their removal today may be an even greater benefit to that public good, yet there is no similar funding source to tap into for their end of life. With their industry long gone, left in place with crumbling abutments, cracked spillways, and leaking foundations, they can become a nuisance and a danger.[13] Property owners may remain liable, but low hazard dams whose failure would have limited impact downstream generally stay under the radar of regulatory agencies. Most high hazard dams in the watershed are owned by local governments. Dams that are lower in height and hazard rating tend to be privately owned, whether by a single homeowner, multiple property owners, or a homeowner association or other such entity.[14] And because it is impractical to monitor or police these effectively, they are generally regarded as nuisance barriers—although for migratory fish, *nuisance* is a word so benign as to be meaningless. These barriers have no easy solutions. Here, the landowners' decision to let the breach go unrepaired is in improvisational accord with the agency's advocacy for dam removal; with the impoundment gone, the water is, after all, flowing once again—though *under* the dam.

Upstream, though, a makeshift pool is taking shape where a colony of beavers has constructed its mansion of logs, sticks, mud, and stones across the stream channel. In a warm spell in early January the emerging pond, though shallow, is brimming with snowmelt and spreading far beyond the banks of the original creek. I had heard in the weeks just after the pond had drained that these eco-engineers would move in quickly, build their dams and their lodges, but the shallow pools that have formed here now look nothing like a millpond. Irregular in shape and depth, they spread out unevenly without any of the tranquil symmetry or reflective calm of a millpond. It's a more haphazard arrangement, a mess, really, but one indicative of structure and reason. Einstein's desk at Princeton, I remember, was famously cluttered and disordered, and I find in these smashed branches, flattened grasses, downed trees an unexpected corollary to his piles of equations, indecipherable messages, and hidden meanings—both of these a kind of genius chaos. Though impenetrable to the rest of us, they suggest a purpose, sense, and logic of their own.

Beavers are a keystone species—that is, one "on which other species in the ecosystem depend"—and the services of these rodent engineers also include creating "new and changing habitats for wildlife and increasing biodiversity."[15] Beaver ponds slow the flow of water. Some of it courses downstream, some evaporates, and some filters into the groundwater. The increased wetland areas will work to filter and remove sediments and pollutants from the water. Their vegetation, shrubs, and roots will also help to absorb snowmelt and rainwater, groundwater and flood waters, releasing the water more gradually into the floodplain and emerging woodland below.[16]

In allowing water to seep into the surrounding wetlands, beavers help to sustain those habitats which more than a third of endangered species depend upon. The ecological complexity of their pooling can generate new habitats for fish, reptiles, aquatic mammals, and birdlife, while the meadows around beaver ponds tend to be nutrient-rich areas that retain seeds. A porous structure that allows for leaks and seepage, the dam still allows the impounded water to offer habitat to snapping and painted and spotted turtles, green frogs, fish, and insects. Beaver ponds are especially beneficial to the blue herons that nest in dead trees behind the impoundment. Ecologists have determined that the water from such wetlands contains fifteen times more plankton and microbial life than those that are beaver free.[17]

Beavers have poor eyesight and often determine the sites of their elaborate construction by listening to the sound of water flow. The buoyancy of their aquatic building sites further helps construction. Still, the speed and volume of water around a beaver dam is ever changing. Beavers shape watersheds and that shape is rarely constant. They may create a single pond or a broad change of interconnected shallow pools. No surprise, then, that a few weeks later after a dry spell, their pond resembles a mudflat, inscribed with a number of thin, trickling rivulets. The rodents have gnawed and toppled both saplings and full-grown trees, destabilizing the banks and exposing them to erosion. For all their instinctive brilliance in construction and deconstruction alike, beavers have never developed that ability to determine the direction in which the trees fall. Their dam is a changing thing, and how it holds, absorbs, and otherwise directs water will vary over time. When rebuilt, it may affect the flow and character of the stream. It may create new wetlands downstream. It's hard to know what shape this place will take.

The way the beavers break up the flow of the stream has led some ecologists to rethink the river continuum concept, amending it to be one of river discontinuum, two words that seem perplexing, even counterintuitive, when coupled. The river continuum concept hasn't always seemed adequate to fully account for the disruptions that can occur within the course of the stream and how these may affect the entire watershed. If the prevailing view is that dams fragment ecosystems and dismantling them allows for stream restoration and the repair of the earth's circulatory system, the idea of river discontinuum suggests instead that the stream is, by nature, a place of interruptions. Along with the barriers constructed by the rodents, natural geological features, sediment flow and deposits, scouring, and the fall line, where rapids and waterfalls mark a change in elevation, have all historically impeded the free flow of waterways. These deviations, intrinsic to ideas of passage, may, in fact, be healthy.[18]

There is a difference between the porousness of a beaver dam and the more substantive barrier of concrete used in water management projects, and I wonder if it's a mistake to use the same word for both types of barriers: One controls water releases, while the other spreads it around, diverting it, shifting its course, allowing it to seep into the earth and saturate it. And I wonder if it is possible to fold this thinking into ideas about river continuum; perhaps the two ideas are mutually compatible. Especially in a time of systems thinking, river ecologists are unlikely to view a waterway as a single fluid entity. It is impossible to consider the health of a waterway without taking in the ecology of its banks, the state of its plant life, the health of the fish and insects for which these provide a habitat, and the inevitable partnership between rush and cessation. Perhaps it is a question of semantics. River continuum theory is described as being longitudinal, and discontinuum theory as more lateral. But disruption, both spatial and temporal, is an inevitable feature of both. And continuity is not unwavering and absolute.

All of which makes me wonder, too, if discontinuum is a part of continuum. I take my question to Stuart Findlay, an aquatic ecologist who has spent more than thirty-five years studying the conditions of the wetlands, shoreline restoration, and water monitoring in the Hudson River watershed. Findlay tells me discontinuity resets continuum; it's like a rest stop on the highway: "You slow down. Or you stop. But the highway keeps on going."[19] And I find myself reconsidering what I know about flow, understanding it now as a changeable phenomenon. The flow of water does not necessarily imply a single direction or steady velocity. It can, in fact, be variable, erratic, multidirectional, lateral as well as longitudinal, inconstant, and unpredictable, a useful fact to consider both near and far from water.

In April, nearly two years after the breach, I look up to see that the old nest, built years ago in the upper reaches of a white pine by a pair of bald eagles, is again occupied. It had remained uninhabited the previous season, but the formidable silhouette of the raptor's domed crown at the nest's rim signals that it is back in operation. Is it presumptuous to think of the eagles' absence as a matter of displacement? Is it the original pair that has come back or its offspring? If it is the original pair, what is it about avian recall that has prompted their return? I know that the memory of birds is spatial rather than sensory, but beyond that, it is hard for me to even imagine the factors governing the eagles' passage back. Do they rely on height, distance, geography, the angle of light, the constellation of stars, the direction of the wind, geomagnetic signals, or instinct? What if we humans had such intrinsic connections to cardinal points, to topography, water, and air? What if we were biologically wired to place? What if our survival relied upon our grasp of such information? What if the skeins of human memory were woven with knowledge of waterways, migratory corridors, air currents, mineral veins, and the slant of sunshine? I try to conceive of what it would be like to navigate my walk using such coordinates, but it is a different cognitive universe, such a fundamentally different and foreign way of organizing experience and information that I am unable to fathom it.

By August, thickets of Japanese knotweed line the path to the floodplain. While songbirds are known to nest in its leaves, the plant doesn't hold soil well and chokes out many other native shrubs. I stand at the end of the old dock and see that shrubs have grown in over the spring and summer; by now the stinging nettles are over my head, and stilt grass, jewelweed, cattails, purple loosestrife, and a purple flower I am unable to identify have all taken root in a chaotic medley of native and nonnative plants. It is all impenetrable, too thick and overgrown to walk through, and even the SEEK app on my phone that can usually identify images of seemingly mysterious plants, insects, amphibians, and more can't seem to make sense of it. It may be a free-for-all that will end up as a forest, though the raging vegetative battle now makes that look unlikely. *Revirescence* is the term of art for renewal, fresh plant growth, emerging greenery that signals the vigor of new life. Certainly it applies here, yet I wonder if there is a twist on the meaning as we use it today. The jumble of local and invasive plants raises questions of what will survive and what will be strangled out in all the new growth. But then, perhaps, renewal is always inherently a matter of what can—and cannot—be predicted.

To try to make sense of how this will all work out, I talk to Laura Wildman, a fisheries and water resources engineer who seems to be the embodiment of a twenty-first-century engineer. With decades of experience in dam removal, fish passage, and river restoration, she is attuned not only to the way structures are put together but to the way they can be broken down. And there is poetic justice in the fact that her office is in Glastonbury, Connecticut, a town on the one area of the Connecticut River where its banks and channels have shifted and meandered constantly throughout history. With the retreat of the last ice sheet, a huge dam of sediment left behind created a vast glacial lake that remained for over 4,000 years. When that dam ultimately gave way, what became the river carved its way through the remaining mud and soft silt, with its channels changing frequently and flooding common.

Wildman's ties to the place don't go back quite that far, but engineering is in her family DNA. Her paternal grandfather was a metallurgical engineer who worked on the Manhattan Project, while her grandfather on her mother's side was a civil engineer who built dams in Arizona, siting dams on horseback. "They would use these plank roads," she tells me. "When they were crossing the desert, they would bring planks and put them down, drive along them, put down more up ahead, and drive a little farther . . ." The sense of ingenuity was contagious, and Wildman admits it was the work of both her grandfathers that led her to a career in engineering. "I was gonna do something like that, build dams, bridges and dams," she tells me, when we meet in a local coffeeshop.

In her late fifties now, Wildman has a direct gaze, and her sense of authority is matched by her enthusiasm for her work. It doesn't hurt that she drives a red pickup truck. She recounts her career with eagerness, not so much because it is her personal story but more because it illustrates changes in the practice of environmental engineering. If it was a discipline largely attentive to sewage and stormwater drainage thirty years ago, today it is just as likely to address the ecology of dam removal, aquatic connectivity, and reestablishing the natural function of waterways, all subjects she remains passionate about today.

Wildman's background is not just a matter of two grandfathers who were engineers. An aunt was a Disney Imagineer, but it was her father's influence as a naturalist that most guided her. He was an avid outdoorsman and would "carry me around on his back in a little basket pack. He would take us canoeing, hiking, tapping maple trees. He read us the *Foxfire* books, stories of people who lived in the Appalachian Mountains," she recalls. "There was nothing romantic or sentimental about these nature stories. They were about resilience and self-reliance—how to make soap, slaughter a pig, make dandelion wine, the natural world as a place presenting challenges and opportunities." She took this perspective with her later as an engineering student at the University of Vermont.

Wildman was two years into a mechanical engineering major before she switched to civil engineering. Even that failed to sustain her interest, and she began to feel increasingly that "engineers have the creativity beaten out of them. They're taught how to fit a design into this box. And politicians love to design boxes. And politicians tend think in political timelines. So we make horrible decisions for the environment when engineers and politicians get together and don't look at geologic timescales and nature timescales and integration of different sciences and concepts. And questioning the restraints you are given. And saying you can't do that. Engineering shouldn't be done that way. You're in a dynamic system and you shouldn't be constructing something there. But the engineer wants the project and is told to build something in this floodplain. And they've been given all these restraints. So they do it. It doesn't allow for the questioning of the entire process and understanding what the best approach would be for that system."

Her voice trails off. "I don't want to turn rivers into Disneyland ecosystems—you look at them there, and it's a concrete-lined canal, not a river. And I knew I wanted to understand those ecological connections and how to restore natural processes." Wildman set out to find the work. It was a time when environmental engineering was a nascent field, and Connecticut's Naugatuck River, long acknowledged as a waterway vital for fish passage, had become so polluted by industry that its color shifted daily. Five dams on the river were up for removal.

Wildman had a grasp of the structural challenges of dam removal. With less knowledge about fish passage, she started researching. "The internet had barely been invented at this point, and we were just at the beginning of email. Everything was brand-new, and there were these things called Listservs. I found a Listserv for fisheries people, the bioengineering section of the American Fisheries Society linking a bunch of emails together." Wildman joined up and asked for information about both dam removal and nature-like fishways, engineered fish passages that resembled the natural flow of waterways. Pioneered in Europe in the 1970s, though used less in the US, their riffles, pools, gradually sloped channels, and gravelly beds both stabilized streambeds and mimicked natural streams more than traditional fish ladders. Senior-level bioengineers around the world responded to her queries with information that came to serve as the basis for her work in environmental engineering, then just an emerging practice. "We got the job working on the Naugatuck River," she says, adding that it was her Damascus moment, teaching her that dam removal could also be a process in holistic river restoration, fish passage, water quality, floodplain management, and riparian planting.

In the years since then, Wildman has worked as a water resources engineer. She has pioneered the complexities of stream management and is clear-eyed about the challenges of nonnative species proliferating today in emerging floodplains. "You've taken an ecology that evolved over hundreds of thousands of years," she explains.

"Before we started to have the anthropogenic impacts on it, there was a dynamic balance because everything is always shifting with species and their interaction and climate and so on. So in order to take out a dam, you're not erasing a lot of other things. But you have to realize all the other things that have gone on in that time too. Development in watersheds, different types of runoff, different temperatures of runoff, different quantities of runoff.

"You've got pockets of various contamination in different places. And introduced species, some that are very invasive and some that have become kind of normalized in the system. We've done so many different things to these systems. So all of a sudden you take out this dam, and it's not like you're turning back history and everything else is the same. You really have to think this through. But even if there are impacts associated with it, the removal of the barriers is always a good idea. You're getting back to where the system can sustain itself. Here in Glastonbury, we are on deposits from a glacial lake. Are we restoring to a pre-glacial lake time? We're not. To me, restoration isn't about some idealized point in time. It's about what we can do now."

What we can do now is an ongoing question at the McKinney floodplain. Earlier in the summer, a crew from Trees for Tribs planted another hundred saplings, and my admiration for the resolve of this young forest is tempered by doubt. The tubes supporting the trees are five feet tall, and before they can be safely removed, the young trees will need to be at least six or seven feet tall, with trunks at least two inches in diameter. It could take the willows four years, the oaks more like six. But my skepticism subsides when I walk the floodplain a couple of months later with George Jackman. In his view it is all nearly utopian. Recalling the pond that had once been there, he said, "You had a desert, and now you have a paradise." You could drink from the creek, he adds, noting that the reinstated wetland predates European settlement. Now there are some loosestrife, grass, sedge, rushes, wild grape, and stinging nettles. The stems of the nettles are covered with sharp prickles that Jackman tells me are good for arthritis. He tells me to try it, and his authority is such that I proceed immediately to rub my hands around the scratchy stems. He's right—it works. He may be a wilderness prophet of sorts, but his constituency is diverse. "People say I am the most hated man in the Hudson Valley," he says. "But the brown trout love me." He finds the floodplain magnificent.

On our walk Jackman mused on biologist Eugene Odum's ideas of ecological succession that speak to how a pond becomes a field, and that a meadow, and that, ultimately, a forest. And while the thicket today is more tangled, dense than ever, I try to remember that it represents a sequence of interconnected events among species that has a logic and order of its own. In Odum's words, what is happening here is not just a succession of species with each acting alone, but a broader developmental process. Ecological succession is the gradual evolution of landscape—of a cornfield abandoned, a floodplain, or a scorched forest—which brings about a change in the ecosystem, in plant species, and in soil. Primary succession occurs in places where there is no soil, as when a glacier retreats and lichen and moss grow in, while secondary succession is what occurs after a disturbance, when one community of plants and animals is replaced by another one altogether, after, say, a fire or a flood.

Odum articulated the idea of ecosystems, the understanding of the natural world "as a system of interlocking biotic communities." I think of that word *ecosystem* and how it has now become a common metaphor for so many things: I've heard it used to describe a tangled network of family relationships, of behaviors in the corporate workplace, of the dynamics of passing legislation in political office, and elsewhere in everything from healthcare to education. It has become the norm to understand the events of ordinary life as a complex system of interconnected circumstances. Which makes sense. Most human beings arrive at some form of this knowledge on their own: you change one thing and you run the risk of pretty much changing everything. Still, I wonder if we have come to accept this idea so readily as a way of making sense of subjects large and small because we have not yet managed to adapt it to our behaviors in the natural world. Will understanding ecosystems as a metaphor help or hinder us in this more crucial grasp of the word? I don't have an answer to that, but on this drizzly summer morning two years after the breach, the waves of Christmas ferns and giant emerald leaves of skunk cabbage colonizing the swamp glisten with beaded moisture, and it is impossible not to acknowledge the simultaneous beauty of landscape and the idea alike.

Beyond thoughts of Odum's theories, the chaos of shrubbery also sent Jackman's thoughts to Macbeth and the branches of Birnam Wood encroaching on the castle. It is a "moving grove," the king's messenger announces, only to be called a liar and a slave by Macbeth. That this floodplain is the chaos of Dunsinane under siege is another way to look at it, and I think of the production designers across theater history who have called for actors carrying boughs to represent an encroaching forest or a gorgeous, raging wave of leaves blowing through an open window. The invading branches are a sign of impending defeat to the king, and beyond that, they signal the instatement of the rightful heir and order restored. How does one convey the idea of a forest moving in? Or the terror of a landscape ceasing to make sense? The human imagination has different ways of comprehending this phenomenon, but still, to see it here now, is something else: a wild beauty that is impassable, impossible, and a transfer, if not of kingdoms then of substance and species, water to land, and a confusion of what is natural and what is unnatural.

The remnants of Hurricane Ida sweeping up through the Northeast in late August 2021 only add to the sense of confusion. The floodplain is again submerged, the contours of the stream indecipherable, rising waters suggesting the pond is on its way back. It is not, of course, but the storm waters have spread out across the plain, flooding it and drowning much of the vegetation, again signaling how quickly water and ground can become one another. It does what a wetland is meant to do: it absorbs and filters high water, renews fish and wildlife habitat, nourishes plant life, and sequesters carbon. The beaver dam upstream looks to have been washed out, at least for now. Possibly it is on its way to becoming a beaver meadow; if its food source is gone, the colony will abandon its pool, leaving behind a nutrient rich area that will eventually grow to brush, then forest.[20] If the food source returns, so too may the rodents. It's difficult to know what this place will be. It's only human to look for certainty, but on this late summer afternoon, it is nowhere to be found.

At the moment this place remains pretty much a mess, which is what it is supposed to be. Assorted types and sizes of plants are crowding each other, but they'll all help to reduce erosion. They'll provide shade, and the insulation and nutrients provided by their leaf litter will benefit organisms that live in the soil. There will be a tangle of understory and overstory. If the beaver pond fills again, minks, muskrats, wood ducks, amphibians, snakes, and wild trout may take up residence. Eels may even return if they can navigate their way past all the other downstream barriers impeding their way. The catfish, crappies, and sunfish, warm water species that flourished in the still pond, will eventually be replaced by those that find habitat in cooler streams, including northern pike, yellow perch, and assorted species of trout.

Three years after the breach, the chaos has subsided. By early fall 2022, the weeds and shrubs in the floodplain include the spiky blossoms of blue vervain, tearthumb, jewelweed, fireweed, polygonum, and native sedge. Six or seven of the saplings planted by the DEC have died, and some of the green protective tubing has been wrenched out of the ground, torn out of position by hard rainfall, wind, and changing water currents. A few of the wooden stakes have likewise been shredded into pieces. Still, most of the saplings are prospering. The polyvinyl tubes have shielded them from deer and invasive plants, and while providing structural support, they also retain heat and moisture to function as mini-greenhouses. The willow saplings especially are flourishing, but other wetland native species—swamp white oak, dogwood, sycamore, red maple—are thriving as well, all of this despite the drought of 2022. But none of it is quite in sync, and the whole place looks like it is in its adolescent phase, all the parts growing at different rates, nothing coming together in any seemingly coordinated way. There is the promise of some eventual order; it may only be ten or so acres, but the emerging woodland reads as new scaffolding for ecological health.

Drawing the moisture up through their trunks, the saplings then release it into the atmosphere through the tiny pores in their leaves. The water is finding its way, part of what Jackman has called "the greatest migration on earth—from clouds, to river, to ocean." Transpiration is the term biologists use to describe one part of that migration, what happens to the water that escapes evaporation and surface runoff, what happens when plants release moisture into the air through their leaves, stems, and flowers, cooling the atmosphere and accessing the carbon dioxide needed for photosynthesis. In cycling that moisture, transpiration is what allows the water to become the cloud, and it's what will make these woodlands active in the ecological exchange between soil, plant, and air. We generally think of plants as absorbing water, but they also determine where water goes and what it does. And trees evaporate more moisture than grasses and shrubs, thus helping to influence weather and climate.[21]

It is also what the poet Tony Hoagland calls *the social life of water* in his poem of that name, imagining that it is a series of such casual encounters that make up the cycle of life:

> All water is a part of other water.
> Cloud talks to lake; mist
> speaks quietly to creek.
>
> Lake says something back to cloud,
> and cloud listens.
> No water is lonely water.

> All water is a part of other water.
> River rushes to reunite with ocean;
> Tree drinks rain and sweats out dew;
> Dew takes elevator into cloud;
> Cloud marries puddle.

Whether you call it transpiration or the social life of water, these saplings are managing it pretty effectively. All of them will also help to stabilize the banks of the new creek.

For now, the beaver pond upstream is going to meadow. It's not clear to me whether the deluge of Hurricane Ida has swept away their constructions or whether they have simply found a better food source elsewhere, but the rodents seem to have vanished, their dam washed out after a series of strong winter rains. The trees they've downed have rearranged the banks and opened the forest canopy, bringing sunlight in. Shrubs and grasses have taken root, and with the impoundment drained, the area is drying out.[22] It's not yet a leafy woodland, and it will take time for the creek to be a cold-water stream. Where water once pooled, there is only marsh, a flatland of smashed grass and fallen oak leaves fringed by some scrubby swamp maples, their buds just coming into their first blush of color now. A thin channel of water not more than fifteen feet wide threads through it quietly, although after a heavy rain even thinner straits of water emerge through the grasses. A silver birch taken down by the beavers a couple of years ago is a relic of their previous enterprise. A few feet away, the bark of a fallen oak has been gnawed off, but not recently. These remnants are surrounded by an overgrowth of brush. Nothing has been near them for a while.

In only several years, the upper pond has gone to floodplain and then to beaver pond, now to marsh and soon to a meadow that will bring species drawn to dry land: deer, rabbits, and foxes. There are black bears in these woods as well. In decades to come, trees will likely be seeded as well, returning this area to woodland. With a new season, the place is just shifting again in its own small story of succession. It's hard not to read in these flattened grasses some lesson about continuum. I'm as open as anyone to valuing the present moment, but this little pool gone to meadow speaks to recognizing incessancy and its inevitability in the next minute, year, decade—and to that elusive alliance between transience and continuity.

Throughout all this change the masonry of the dam remains in place, useless now, an incidental monument to a bygone enterprise. For all the solidity of the edifice, its inadequacy is evident as water continues to stream beneath its foundational stonework. Eventually it could present logistical problems. Heavy rains could transform the wetland back to a pond, and high water could put extreme pressure on the already compromised dam. "Anything manmade always requires maintenance," says Brian Scoralick, executive director of the county's soil and water conservation district. "It'll cause problems eventually, and a hands-off approach is not always the best."

It's a May afternoon nearly four years after the breach and we're taking in the site. Scoralick is tall, over six feet, with a strong jawline, steady gaze, and sense of command that may also come from his profession; he carries himself as someone accustomed to managing earth, bodies of water, stonework. Yet if his presence is innately imposing, he wears it lightly. More than once in our conversation he talks of taking a hybrid approach to conservation. This is no doubt an asset, because he is often in the position of working on the same site with different constituencies and varying interests, among them NYSDEC, other state agencies, regional environmental groups, municipalities, and private landowners. Local to the area, he remembers his own astonishment at how the dam breached in a matter of hours.

Now he looks at the fast-growing junk weeds growing on the banks, the flowering honeysuckle, the long, tapered leaves of ailanthus, the barberry. "Hopefully, it won't turn into a jungle," he says of the chaos. When he turns to look at the dam, he is more confident. "The connection is already there," he says, meaning that the breach has already joined two sections of the tributary, albeit unintentionally. The risk now is less ecological, he suggests, and more one of a strong storm requiring an emergency response or causing damage to the bridge spanning the creek just a few feet south of the dam.

He points out the stream's *thalweg*, a word new to me. Derived from the German, it means "the way of the valley." It's a thick, clumsy mouthful that sounds nothing like what it means, which is the line of lowest elevation in running water, that place where the water is deepest and fastest flowing, an axis, a wire, a vein, a fuse, a ribbon within the quick current that defines the stream's natural direction. Where the channel runs straight, the thalweg is generally in the middle of the waterway; at a bend, it will shift to the outside edge. Changeable as it may be, it is still often used to determine the most navigable area of a river and to serve as a boundary in legal matters of property ownership. For all its import, it is barely visible here, appearing to be nothing more than a slight midstream riffle. I marvel at the way something so decisive can appear so slender, be so fluid. And at how this thin thread of water can mark such a certain path at a moment when so many facts and events of the natural world are so deeply uncertain.

It's a truism in stream ecology that all dams will come down: They'll either fail or be brought down intentionally. This dam seems to be a monument marking some accidental middle ground. Although it has certainly failed, it remains solidly in place, the water streaming through its base attesting to its inadequacy. Yet it functions as a kind of grade control for the creek, and its removal could require a realignment of the channel. Likewise, if the bridge that spans the creek just below the dam were to wash out, the creek's path would also shift. Scoralick suggests that a compromise approach might make sense here: Bring the dam down by several feet. This would allow for fish passage while letting the dam continue to function as grade control. "Climate intelligence" is the newly coined term that describes emerging knowledge with which to manage the risks and dangers brought about by climate change. This dam—still in place, leaking, obsolete, but in its own incidental manner allowing the stream to flow freely while tempering its grade—is an apt example for the conundrums much of the built world reflects at this time and exactly the kind of site that asks for such intelligence.

Average global temperatures in the summer of 2023 were the highest in recorded history. Evidence from ice cores, tree rings, fossils, lake sediments, and other more rudimentary tools of temperature measurement suggested to some scientists that these were the warmest days on earth since the last ice age, 125,000 years ago. In the Hudson Valley, brown spongy moths swarm the air around the pond, part of an early summer infestation that has defoliated trees on the hillside just west of the creek. The trees are likely to recover, but what does a summer of leafless trees do to the food chain? Throughout the season, there were also days when the skies were thick with an orange haze, a product of smoke plumes from Canadian wildfires. How do these new fire seasons and the fine particle air pollution they produce affect insects? Birds? Early research suggests that smoke endangers the respiratory system of birds, disrupting their migration patterns. In mid-July, a summer storm delivers some five inches of rain in a single night, the most intense storm since Ida two years earlier. Both have been designated "1000-year storms," an aberration that New York State Governor Kathy Hochul calls the new normal. The channel has vanished in the surge of milky, chocolate brown floodwaters, recalling the old pond, though with banks and edges less certain. While the dam holds some water back, much of it is roiling, turbulent, and surging through beneath.

Such is the unexpected and seemingly random constellation of events in a single summer that are impossible to predict. How will these dissonances affect the emerging woodland? In a time of such uncertainty, how do scientists even know how to frame their research? How is it even possible to plan the growth of a forest? I think again about Scott Cuppett's words. The channel changes. The shape of silt and the movement of water changes over time. Wait it out. See what happens. Maybe it's enough to know that now. Let the sediment shift. Let the creek find its own path. I've found myself repeating this directive often to myself in conditions that exist well outside of this floodplain: a conversation, an argument, a silence, occurrences that have some equivalence to a tuft of grass matted down by rain, a sapling bent, a bit of earthen bank reconfigured or water turning to air. And I know by now as well that the sinuosity, the oxbow, the braiding, and the curves of the creek are a sign of its health. These natural bends are necessary. The direct and linear path forward is something we humans have been taught to value. Here, though, is evidence that the circuitous route offers its own logic and grace.

In early August 2023, after things have dried out a bit, a team from Riverkeeper, Trout Unlimited, and Trees for Tribs show up to do some annual maintenance on the saplings—straightening the tubes, removing those that are no longer needed, firming up the plants, and driving stakes deeper into the ground. Rogue stakes and tubes are scattered about, and many of the tubes left standing have an accumulation of silt both inside and out that hasn't helped the plants inside much. Desiccated brown stalks poke through some of the tubes, while flourishing trees and shrubs emerge from others. The plants hit hardest are those closer to the defunct dam, where the water pooled and eddied before surging through the base.

Beth Roessler, Tributary Conservation Specialist for the Hudson River Estuary Program at NYSDEC, is organizing the effort this morning, and I ask her about the effect on the saplings of the spongy moth caterpillars that have nibbled on entire forests of oak and other hardwoods earlier in the summer, defoliating them and leaving them susceptible to disease. Not a forester, she's not sure, and more than once over the course of the morning, she prefaces her answers to my questions with, "I'm not an expert, but . . ." Now she tells me she suspects that the moths don't attack smaller plants as vigorously as they do mature trees. "But that doesn't mean it didn't happen," she says. Roessler has been at this a long time and works with a sense of humility; she knows what she doesn't know, which in its own way advances her sense of authority. She's clear on what she is doing and works with efficiency. Her hair is held in a long braid behind her back, and she puts every pocket and belt loop to use with knife, clippers, zip ties, gloves, and all the other necessary tools of the day. When she readjusts a bent tube over a black willow, clipping off a few rogue bits, her hands are sure. Just as confidently, she dispatches a dead red maple sapling but leaves a red oak; there is a "tiny, tiny chance its roots are still alive."

Roessler's ease with uncertainty evokes Barry Lopez's essay, "The Naturalist," in which he notes a shift in our search for knowledge in the natural world. It may no longer be enough to simply know all there is to know about a single organism or even species. Rather, there is a need to understand broader relationships, connections, associations, what he calls a growth of awareness: "To get anywhere deep with a species, you must immerse yourself in its milieu. . . . She or he knows a local flora and fauna as pieces of an inscrutable mystery, increasingly deep, a unity of organisms. . . . The modern naturalist has become a kind of emissary, working to establish good relations with all the biological components humanity has excluded from its moral universe."

After the breach, though dozens of native cottonwoods took root, few of the seedlings have survived, questioning again the sense in depending on native species to adapt. It would be nice to be able to count on natural regeneration, Roessler says, but it's difficult on a site like this. While bathometric studies of the pond and its bed might have helped to determine which plants would best prosper here, the breach happened too quickly to allow for that. You can't predict everything. The stream remains unstable, the soil unconsolidated, and the soft silt of its bed continuing to shift over time. The western side of the creek, where a number of sycamores and maples are thriving, is at an elevation about a foot higher than the eastern side—not much, but enough to make a big difference in soil content. The excessive moisture on the eastern side was such that plant roots easily rotted.

Yet I know by now that some of the crew have taken to calling the scraggly floodplain "McKinney Forest," which expresses a clear sense of expectation. After a couple of hours, the team has removed some sixty tubes. Although some have been taken from flourishing plants that no longer need protection, many are removed from those that haven't made it. None of it comes as a surprise or is considered a failure. There was no sure path for the stream's meander to take. It kept shifting. It was all an experiment, Roessler says: "We put in a lot of different species just to see. We just wanted to find out what would work."

And what works continues to reveal itself over time. Water continues to stream beneath the dam, though it floods and pools behind the dam after intense rains. The sediment saturated and softened from such periodic deluge can weaken the plants, and not all can take root. While the alders and willows manage to adapt, as do the sycamores on just slightly higher ground, the oaks and maples closer to the creek are struggling. In allowing for recurring inundation, the dam remains a controlling influence, and only about a quarter of the trees planted have made it. The others have gotten knocked down, uprooted. Cattails, purple loosestrife, jewelweed, stilt grass, and a medley of other native and nonnative weeds and bushes proliferate.

But still, there is none of the knotweed that is flourishing elsewhere in the neighborhood, and after a visit the following fall, Matt Best, a habitat restoration manager at Riverkeeper, calls the wildflowers, grasses, and shrubs a welcoming pollinator sanctuary for the nesting sites, shelter, nectar sources, and pollen they offer to birds, moths, beetles, butterflies, and other insects.[23] And in that way we have come to celebrate events that are small yet momentous, a twelve-second iPhone video documents a tube being ripped and the stakes removed from a thriving maple sapling. "Liberated Tree," the credit reads.

"It's a varying ecosystem," George Jackman says when I reach him by phone. "The creek has said 'not yet.'" And after a pause: "It's still a transition area. And it's still a beautiful place." I know there is some conversation about planting more saplings in the floodplain upstream, another experiment as the stream continues to find its path. Jackman's words remind me that wishing on trees is a time-honored human imperative, whether it is the cathedral reach in a forest of eastern pines or the massive trunk and wide canopy of a centuries-old oak. The wish tree is a common symbol in eastern spiritual practice; with roots that run deep, branches spread wide and alive with birdsong, the divine arboreal species is a symbol of prosperity, a source of wisdom, and a place of shelter in both Buddhist and Hindu philosophy.

The emerging grove now suggests some contemporary manifestation of that, but here the subject of hope is the tree itself, the protective tubing around it underscoring the fragility of such desires. For now, maybe it's enough to understand that the transition is continuing, an intrinsic and ongoing change in character that takes this little patch of place from millpond to creek, from reflective pool to moving water, from stillness to flow. I remember that a tributary can be defined as a contributing factor in something that happens. What was once a millpond is on its way to being a woodland—maybe of red, sugar, and silver maples; of river birch, ironwood, blue beech, black gum, white pine, sycamore, black willow, smooth alder, and silky dogwood. Or maybe a composition of willows, sycamores, and maples. Its final arrangement remains unknown. If it is a succession of uncertainties, it still speaks to that possibility that one thing *can*—genuinely, deeply, truly—become something else entirely, an idea I find strangely and unexpectedly sustaining on a deeper human level.

Figure 4. Rocks and riffles are part of the restored stream at what was once Shapp Pond.

The Creek Restored

Shapp Pond Dam

Dams have a very complicated inner life.

—Werner Herzog[1]

The view from a bridge to the water below is almost always mesmerizing. Maybe it's the very idea of flow, of movement, of inevitability, of inexorable change that so engages us, but there is something about holding still while watching the stream beneath that calls to the human imagination. That sense of continuity is welcome today at the East Branch of the Wappinger Creek in Salt Point, New York. Although the winter of 2021 has seen little snowfall, temperatures have been frigid, and on an early spring morning the sense of flow and momentum in the rushing water seems promising. A few hundred feet upstream, the creek runs with quiet certainty, but when it approaches the bridge and the adjacent spot where a grist mill once stood, it takes a small bend, becomes riffled, churned up by fallen trees and logs and exposed rocks. A bit of gravelly sand flat protects the quiet water in a tiny inlet just below the old millhouse on the eastern bank. That minor disruption in flow is a result of the slight shift in its course, a revision in the shape of its bed and banks made in 2016 when a small dam that was once part of the mill was disassembled and removed.

The mill and turbine powering it were built in the late 1700s in the hamlet of Hibernia by David Arnold. He is described as a "disowned Quaker" with a "litigious and aggressive manner," but must have been as enterprising as he was difficult, building both the mill and adjacent bridge that allowed local farmers and merchants to access it. After about a dozen years and some undocumented transgression, Arnold outlived his welcome in the Quaker community settled there and left the property. The mill and several others nearby remained thriving, prosperous in processing textiles, wood, grains, and cider through the late nineteenth century, when the regional economy shifted. Industrialization in manufacturing and the arrival of the railroad then allowed local merchants and craftsmen to exchange goods with a broader public and residents to purchase products not produced in the immediate neighborhood.[2] A black-and-white postcard from the 1930s shows the dam with the caption, "Electric Power Plant, Clinton Corners," documenting the shift in the enterprise to a source for hydroelectricity, though for how long remains unclear: The rush of water pictured attests to the power source, but the little farmhouse and barn on the adjacent grassy hillside offer a more bucolic image of an energy plant than any we might have today.

The dam and its waterfall remained in place, though, and a century later the old millhouse became a residence. While cedar shingles sheathe the upper floors of the building, the foundation and lower walls are built of stone to withstand the rise and rush of water. Until 2016, the millpond had been outfitted with a little dock, a boat. On my first visit there in January 2021, I'd met with the property owner, Hilary Kliros, an art director whose full-time residence is in New York City. The Covid-19 virus was coursing through the country, so we stood outdoors wearing masks as she gestured towards the abutments and the area where the dam once stood. She also handed me a stack of photographs from that time, and I leafed through images ranging from impressionistic views of water, sunlight, the reflections of shadow and leaves to others that captured the structure itself more explicitly: the crumbling concrete, the rush of the waterfall, a floating dock and a ladder, and the quiet summer pond shaded by trees where she and her family could drift in an old rowboat or paddle a few hundred feet upstream.

The dam was gone now, but other vestiges of the pond spoke with eloquence to the history of the place. Its old concrete abutments had been left in place on either side of the creek, pitted and scarred ruins blanketed in moss and lichen, remnants of industrial archeology that did not look out of place. More subtle was the old waterline along the stream, eight or ten feet above the surface of the creek. Although it had been five years since the dam was removed, only a few scattered shrubs were growing there. Closer to the house, Kliros and her husband had planted a little ledge of grass, a terrace of sorts, just above the creek.

As we are chatting there, something fast, sleek, dark darting through the leaves and branches along the shore catches my eye, and I realize it is a mink scampering along the brush on the shore. Minks are comfortable in cold water habitats, but the still waters of the millpond had not been accommodating. With the dam gone, they can thrive along the cooler rocky stream threading its way through the woodland, making their dens somewhere along the banks, beneath the tree roots, along the tumble of rocks and logs. I ask what other species have arrived since the dam was removed. "Fewer worms, more flying bugs," her husband, Dan, tells me.

The dam's removal had been a matter of both habitat restoration and safety. Nearly seventy-five feet long and some twelve feet high, it was pinned on bedrock. Its amalgam of poured concrete and stonework is what is called Cyclopean concrete, an antique technique in which large stones are put into place as the concrete is poured. An improvised construction typical of its time, its masonry was further shored up by pieces of miscellaneous scrap metal, old tools, pitchforks, barrel straps, reinforcement rods, and other found bits and pieces. Over the decades, though, leaks had developed, and water flowed around and under the dam. Generations of wear had compromised its structural integrity, and in the 1950s, the top four feet of it had become destabilized and tumbled into the water below, where the pieces remain today, a few refrigerator-size chunks still visible above the water line. Ad hoc efforts to seal the dam included applying a steel wire fence mesh to the upstream face of the dam, and parging it with cement mortar. The mortar never bonded to the dam, soon separating in sheets, and the repair only added to the dam's overall state of deterioration.

Heavy rains from Tropical Storm Irene in 2011 had caused the creek to swell, loosening stones in the foundation further, and water began to flow beneath them, undermining the entire structure. At one point, Dan tells me, he had waded into the creek and used a fifteen-foot sapling pole to probe the bed of the creek near the upstream face of the dam. The pole never touched bottom, suggesting the depth of the chasm beneath the dam that was allowing water to surge through. The breach could possibly allow for some limited fish migration: Any break in a dam can offer an upstream path to aquatic species, and eels especially are slippery, resourceful creatures that can find their way through weird slips and cracks. That said, such breaks are not adequate for substantive passage, and leaving a barrier in place never answers to the realities of fish migration.

Although it was part of the naturally narrow channel, the millpond above the spillway was loaded with 150 years of silt, sediment, trash, tools, old car parts, trees, limbs, and assorted other debris that all applied further pressure on the dam. A ravine upstream had served as a garbage dump for decades, and after high water the rubbish washed downstream, its further passage obstructed by the dam. Drenched mattresses, plastic bottles, an old bicycle, fishing gear, windows, a couple of toilet bowls had all collected there, evidence of the time-honored rural tradition of using the stream as a junkyard. In its current state, the dam had become a safety hazard for Kliros, her family, and their neighbors downstream. Like other outdated industrial mill dams that slow the current of the stream, this one had helped to raise water temperature and lower dissolved oxygen levels, leading to occasional algae blooms in the impounded water. Now those dangers had multiplied: While the millpond continued to drain through the breach at its base, the concrete structure also continued to trap and hold debris. In what engineers call "failure mode," the dam was at risk of simply sliding out during high water or going into bending failure.

Kliros had inherited the millhouse, pond, and property around it from her mother, Thea Kliros, a fashion illustrator and award-winning children's book illustrator, who bought the house in the mid-1980s, falling in love with it on her first drive past. After Thea Kliros died in 2013, her daughter found herself, just as her mother had, receiving frequent notices from engineers at the New York State DEC Division of Water about her accountability as the landowner of a property with a dam in a state of imminent failure. The structure's deficiencies were catalogued as "seepage, slope stability, undesirable growth, maintenance, surficial deterioration, voids, and cracking." More general remarks alluded to fissures on the downstream face, the wash of sediment, and water flow under the dam. "If this dam is no longer serving an important function, we suggest you consider removing it," the letter continued. Nothing in the wording was threatening, but the correspondence came by certified mail with return receipt requested, and its message was clearly more than a suggestion.

Like most private landowners finding themselves facing the dangers associated with owning a dam, along with insurance and liability costs, Kliros was without the ready resources to cover the upwards of $150,000 for the permitting fees, engineering plans, deconstruction, and landscape restoration costs such a project would require. And like most private dam owners, she hadn't fully grasped the responsibilities, the repairs, the hazards such ownership brought with them. Still, in an effort towards compliance, she requested an engineer's report in 2014 which confirmed that with the volume of water flowing through its base, the level of the water above and below the dam had become equalized, "disappearing" the pond. In sedate prose, the report spoke to the gravity of the situation: "A turbulent area on the upstream face of the dam and an area of eddying on the downstream face in line with the upstream turbulence, indicating that water had eroded a channel beneath the dam. This channel has sufficient area to carry the stream flow during normal periods." And then, in conclusion: "Some measure must be taken to either stabilize or remove this dam before a catastrophic breaching occurs during high flow conditions."

In her mid-sixties, Kliros has a slight frame and delicate features, neither of which undermines her innate sense of tenacity and resolve. She conveys the sensibility of someone who wants to do the right thing, along with the casual confidence to manage it. Both qualities were put to test in the subsequent three years as she formed a partnership with local town and planning boards; the Dutchess County Soil and Water Conservation District, which conducted engineering, demolished the dam, and worked to restore the banks; NYSDEC; and the Hudson River Estuary Program. When I ask her in one of our subsequent meetings how this alliance actually came into being, her eyes don't quite glaze over, but she murmurs that she has forgotten many of the details in much the way of someone who has endured exhaustive experience—one that includes information overload, emotional fatigue, financial panic, and resolving a vast range of human interests that are in inevitable conflict with one another—forgets as much as she possibly can as soon as she can. She is not given to hyperbole, but it is a form of amnesia that others given to greater drama might legitimately attribute to post-traumatic stress.

Still, she passes over a stack of over a dozen file folders containing copies of permits, emails, grant applications, correspondence with regulatory agencies, spreadsheets, notes from the town board, construction estimates, documents for liability insurance, engineering drawings, site plans, site photographs, daily work reports, miscellaneous leaflets about protecting streambanks, environmental assessment forms, a list of suggested buffer trees and shrubs for shoreline planting, and more. Handwritten notes, business cards, sticky notes in all colors slip in and out of the folders. I know from our conversations that she is organized and clear thinking and that the files have an innate logic and order to them, but the piles of labyrinthine paper work seem obscure, difficult to follow, even a little chaotic, and the tone of the correspondence ranges at times from frustration to outright despair. "It was a little nightmarish, and I cried more than once," she told me, a statement which I come to suspect is colossal understatement.

In January 2016, NYSDEC developed its grants program, allocating nearly $400,000 to be administered by the Hudson River Estuary Program to promote coastal resiliency and aquatic habitat. The East Branch of the

Wappinger Creek is a major tributary to the Hudson and drains an area of about eight-five square kilometers, and the derelict dam disrupted flow, degraded water quality, and prevented fish migration. Imperiled by extreme storms and the potential for flooding, the dam was also obviously a safety hazard. All of this designated it as an obvious candidate for removal, and $96,408 was awarded to the project. With further funding forthcoming from the New York State Water Resources Institute to allow researchers from Cornell University to monitor and collect data about the site's aquatic and riparian habitats, Kliros was in a position to move forward.

Because the water level had already been lowered by the earlier breach at the base of the dam, there was no impounded water to be released. That breach had also allowed much of the sediment from the impoundment to flow downstream, eliminating the need for a spoils area. In the five years since Hurricane Irene's visit, sediment had been redistributed down to the mouth of the river and possibly beyond. Still, there were remnants of storm damage, massive tree limbs and branches, and a good amount of organic debris to be hauled away. So as not to create an undue degree of turbidity, NYSDEC advocated for dam removal in "dry conditions," certainly a euphemism considering the task at hand. Because installing a backhoe in the streambed itself would have been unjustifiably invasive, two choices offered themselves: the stream flow could be redirected and diverted around the dam, or a piping system and pump could be put in place upstream to redirect the water away from the removal site.

Engineers opted for the second choice. Because the old stone and clapboard millhouse was built directly above the eastern bank of the creek, construction would take place on the western bank. And then, in late summer 2016, the Dutchess County Soil and Water Conservation District, working with engineers and consultants, began deconstruction. That the dam was precarious and in a state of disrepair was not without advantages. The channel above the dam was cut off with two temporary sandbag coffer dams. Two massive portable pumps, capable of diverting thousands of gallons of water per minute away from the original channel, were installed, along with a diversion pipe twenty-four inches in diameter placed in the old sluice gate to manage stream flow during construction. In a little more than three weeks, the dam was dismantled piece by piece, the concrete cut up into manageable rubble that was then hauled up the bank and loaded into trucks for removal. Dead trees, along with the years' worth of upstream debris that by now also included miscellaneous auto parts, window frames, an old bicycle, and the remains of a racoon were hauled off as well. The coffer dams and pumps were removed, and the bed of the old millpond was reconfigured to conform to the channel.

Predictably, the assorted parties had priorities that were often at odds with one another. Even the most fastidious ecologists can disagree, depending on whether they are protecting the interests of water, plants, air, or animal species. When the engineers and DEC advocated for a temporary dirt road to be constructed so that heavy equipment could access the removal site, for example, town board members took issue with the number of trees that would need to be removed. The area designated for heavy construction equipment was also a steep slope, requiring its own special permit. Without background as an on-site general construction contractor, Kliros often found herself having to negotiate such disputes, all of which raises the question: If removing these antiquated structures is of such urgent ecological concern, is there not a more efficient and logical way to structure the permitting process and the work at large?

While the bedrock on the floor of the creek helped to stabilize the new waterway, the engineers took depth and width measurements of both upstream and downstream channels, then mimicked those to shape the new one. Because the relatively narrow width of the millpond itself was consistent with the width of the stream above it, there was no extensive reconfiguration. A thin zone of riprap, loose stone used to stabilize riverbanks, was laid down above the abutments on both sides of the creek to help forestall erosion, a bit of hardscaping, but not enough to create a hardened channel. The water was then permitted to resume its flow. Left in place, the area around the rocks has now filled in with soil. The newly charted stream course allowed for some elements of the old structure to be preserved, and the abutments that remain in place today reference the site's history while framing the recontoured channel. Photographs taken of the site after the final week of construction show a stretch of cloudy gray-green water flowing between the abutments. While not especially clear, the upper and lower streams are full, flowing, finally reconnected.

Hilary has let me look through the daily work reports made by the construction team. If I'm looking for the Hallelujah moment when the last piece of concrete is removed and the dam finally dismantled, I don't find it. "CV had a sub-contractor performing the cutting of the existing dam. The crew had set up a pulley system on the east side of the dam and was using a diamond studded line to cut the dam from the bottom upwards," reads an entry from August 17. And the following day: "The sub contractor had just finished cutting the concrete dam upon LTC arrival." It's all in a day's work, and the straightforward account a reminder that momentous events are sometimes best conveyed best with blunt candor and accuracy. But leafing further through the files, I come across an email from Scott Cuppett. I know by now that he is generally given to drier and more technical language, but here his terseness in summing up the project is underscored by his restrained exhilaration: "Another dam bites the dust . . . eels benefit."

A reconfigured waterway necessitates a reconfigured shoreline, preferably one that will reduce erosion, filter water, and trap sediment. A number of trees on the steep, wooded western hillside of the creek had been cut down and removed to allow for heavy construction equipment to reach the site. Afterwards, the hillside was graded, and erosion control matting was put down on disturbed areas to hold the topsoil in place until vegetation could take root. Seeds for streamside grasses and shrubs were planted along with mulch to stabilize the bank. Later, some forty saplings, largely native red and gray dogwood, were planted through the Trees for Tribs program. A liminal rocky area between the water and the hillside was planted with shrubs, but the soil there has washed away, leaving the plantings sparse. Nothing here is a quick fix.

In the years following, the Department of Natural Resources at Cornell University prepared its own report on the effects of the dam removal, gathering data about fish and macroinvertebrate species for three years both above and below the dam to determine the ecological consequences. Species diversity, habitat, and water quality had all benefited. Sediment absorbs heat, thereby warming the water, but now much of the sand and silt that had accumulated behind the dam has been washed downstream, leaving a habitat composed mostly of cobble and gravel. When a dam comes out, those bits of sand and small gravel that have been collecting behind the structure migrate downstream, allowing invertebrates and small fish to take refuge in the tiny interstitial spaces. It allows for species richness, and the thriving population of mayflies, caddisflies, and stoneflies gives credence to Dan's notice of "more insects."

When I reach him on the phone, Jeremy Dietrich, an aquatic ecologist in the Department of Natural Resources and the Environment at Cornell University, tells me the stream may have been restored to something close to its original channel, what he calls "the preferred lotic stream condition." The 500-year storms that now regularly visit this area flush out the stubborn silts and clay, in the process also whisking away the tiny invertebrates that make their habitat there. It's yet another paradox of stream restoration: Flushing out the sand and silt keeps the waterway dynamic and healthy, but a sudden rush of high water can also scour the streambed in a manner detrimental to invertebrates.

Fish species that thrive in cool water, generally defined as below seventy or seventy-five degrees, include brown trout, eastern blacknose dace, and longnose dace, and these have flourished, while warm water species such as white suckers, bluegill sunfish, and brown and yellow bullheads diminished. "The fish were just knocking at the door," says Ryan Coulter, an aquatic biologist at the DEC working on the data. "The dam comes down and now they're free to roam." Coulter also tells me the rapid three-year recovery time hadn't surprised him, which is worth noting. In environmental work, finding quantifiable results so quickly is not the norm; we are more accustomed to timeframes that work in reverse of this: an oil spill, say, that in minutes and hours contaminates a body of water that takes decades to clean. But the benefits of dam removal, if not immediate, are fast, and when a pond is returned to a free-flowing reach, restoration is imminent.

With the removal restoring upstream access to about five miles of the creek's east branch for both migratory and resident fish species, the Shapp Pond project was cited by NYSDEC as a success story in early 2020. While Kliros had invested close to $50,000 of her own into the removal, over $96,000 from the Hudson River Estuary Grants program and $33,000 from the New York State Water Resources Institute had covered the costs of engineering, demolition, and shoreline restoration, along with the subsequent monitoring and data collection of aquatic species and habitat. Literature accompanying the announcement cited that "the formerly impounded section of the East Branch of the Wappinger Creek now supports aquatic life uses," crediting foremost the collaboration between Kliros, the local soil and water conservation district, and the Hudson River Estuary Program.

As Kliros walks me through the history of the project in a wide-ranging conversation, we discover that we both went to the same college—and that our mothers both attended that college as well. It seems almost ridiculous to me, too obvious, this coincidence of connections making itself clear as we stand above a stream that has itself become an exhibit of connectivity, its channel restored. It would be absurd to look for such explicit concurrences between our lives and the natural world, but it's hard not to take notice when they occur. And I remember that by happenstance, I had made my visit to the creek on New Year's Day, 2021. There was something then in this view to continuity and forward momentum that felt auspicious, a sense of release and possibility. I look again now at the abutments left at the edge of the water and the little creek coursing between them. It's flowing fast with certainty and assurance and, not for the first time, I think that sometimes the best we can do is get ourselves and our things out of the way.

Creative thinking in the early twenty-first century may have as much to do with how we take things apart as with how we put them together; disassembly as much as assembly; deconstruction as much as construction; shaping absence as well as presence. We know now that how manufactured things—whether a chair, a tire, or a laptop—can be broken down for recycling is as important to their overall design as how they serve their original purpose. Habitat for Humanity, along with its program for building and restoring houses, also offers deconstruction and demolition services. As profligate consumers of products, energy, resources, we have overmade, overbuilt, and overused. Deacquisition may be as important in our relations to the material world as acquisition. And it occurs to me that the little glossy mink scrambling through the brush that I saw here on my first visit may serve as a good mascot for this deconstruction.

There could be others as well. In an email Kliros sent to the partnership after completion of the project, she wrote, "The stream is now so beautiful and magical, it keeps shifting and changing. . . . and from my living room window I can see so many creatures enjoying it, turtles, possums, beavers and herons . . . and I'm sure many more hidden from my sight." Her words remind me that the hour-to-hour, day-to-day ordinary experience of the stream's shifting character is a form of data collection too. And her last four words are also a reminder that the rewards of such work *are* often unseen, an obvious point perhaps, but still one worth noting in a hyper-visual age.

After our initial visit in 2021, Kliros had invited me to swing by anytime and she showed me where to park up the road. And so from time to time, I do. Sometimes my visits to the site are just a quick drive-by, but other times I stop and get out of the car. On a winter visit, I find a gallery of still forms: a frosting of snow settled on the abutments, a film of razor-thin ice fringing the quiet water at the edges of the creek, ice crystals glistening on the exposed stones. Elsewhere, rocks of frozen snow have collected against a fallen tree limb. Midstream, though, the creek itself is a dark rush of winter water. And there's something else: This little bit of the stream flows north, a direction that seems counterintuitive and only adds to a sense of things being not what you'd expect. I know by now that the curves, bends, and otherwise circuitous routes the stream takes are a sign of its health. Yet water flowing north always seems a little off to me, intuitively weird, and I am reminded again of the flawed nature of my own expectations, not a bad thing to know when you are trying to watch something closely.

A few weeks later, after the snow has melted, I swing by again. It is a warm day in March. The grass on the hill is just greening, the dogwood trees soon to bud. A collection of logs and branches has been washed downstream and is caught now in a tumble of rocks, creating their own little improvisational blockade. The water bubbles and eddies. I know that streams conform to a dynamic process and all these minor obstructions serve a purpose, creating rills and riffles that shape tiny habitats in the rocks and substrate and bring oxygen into the water, helpful to fish and insects. Surface water flows more quickly than the water at the bed, which is slowed by the friction from stones, silt, and organic matter. Fish can lay their eggs in the gravel beds, while the deeper pools nurture larger species.[3] Free-flowing creeks move faster than those that are intermittently dammed, and that sense of energy is here. And if the creek bank may seem a little messy with its haphazard arrangement of leaves, rocks, branches, it's the kind of mess that signals things are moving along just as they should.

When I visit later in the summer, after the flooding caused by hurricanes Henri and Ida, the area that had once been a millpond remains now a quiet, shallow pool. Kliros had emailed me photographs of the creek during the storms, and I could see that the surge of muddy water had reached the level of the old mill pond and was lapping at the upper edge of the stones marking the small, grassy terrace the family built after the dam had been removed. The gravel island where I once saw a mink had been washed over, but the high water was accommodated, and it's hard not to wonder how the dam would have withstood the two consecutive storms.

Just downstream, the stream is still flowing fast and full, its gravel bed carved with new, thin tributaries. The grass and weeds growing on the bank have been smashed flat by the high water, and rocks in the creek bed roughen up the waters, creating rills. A new arrangement of branches and tree trunks has been caught up at the bend, creating a porous barrier that the water rushes through, over, and around. The falls and riffles bring oxygen, vital to the habitat of cold stream species, into the churned-up water.[4] The vegetative cover and saplings have kept the upper bank from eroding, but little else here is static. Later, in November, the creek is carrying a quiet parade of oak leaves downstream. A tiny gravel beach just below the remains of the old abutment is full of washed-up tree limbs and piles of leaves. The place is constantly reshaped, but every time I go, it offers a view to water that is unhindered, free-flowing. There is something ordinary about water just following its course, a sense of affirmation of things getting where they need to be; casual, ordinary progress, life moving on irrevocably as it is meant to do.

By coincidence, the house across the road from the millhouse and part of the hamlet's early creek-side settlement, is one my husband and I had considered buying many years earlier when we had been looking to move to the area. Now whenever I drive along the crooked little road to the millhouse and bridge, it's the first signpost I look for, the small colonial clapboard house where we almost lived. Just as the upstream and downstream sections of the creek are connected with one another, the proximity of the little house to the restored stream speaks to the confluence of lives chosen and those refused, both essential to who we become, and over time this little tableau of continuity becomes a place where my lived life converges with my imagined life.

Over the course of months, Kliros emails me photos of the stream before and after, and I browse through them: the dam in winter, its waterfall both frozen and flowing; a picture of Kliros's young daughter drifting in an inner tube in the pond, her fingers trailing the water; another image that captures the surge of the waterfall framed by the mullions of an upstairs window. I wonder what it would like to have this curtain of rushing water as constant and daily scenery. A photograph taken from the opposite side of the stream just after the dam has been removed captures the newly planted grassy area below the millhouse: The trees and shrubs have not yet grown in. The bit of stony riprap lines the shore to protect it from any erosion and scouring that might occur before the plantings grow in. A single blue lawn chair has been positioned at the edge of the creek.

It's been seven years since the dam was removed, and Hilary, Dan, and I are sitting in an area that serves as kitchen and living room. As in so many eighteenth-century houses, the rooms are small, but the scale is comfortable—this one has painted floorboards, a cushioned window seat, a table piled with books. A ferocious gray squirrel taxidermied by Hilary and Dan's daughter when she was a teenager is creeping down one wall, but that's not the only way the outdoors is coming in. The millhouse was built for and around the water, and its contiguity with the stream below is part of its character. Even 250 years later, the house and the stream seem inseparable, two parts to a single whole, and it was easy to see why Kliros's mother had fallen in love with the house on her drive-by forty years earlier.

I ask Hilary how her family's experience of the house has changed over the years they have lived there, from the time it overlooked a placid millpond and waterfall to its current proximity to a free-flowing stream; and what it has been like to go from a house overlooking fast-flowing water to one beside a quiet meandering stream. She looks out the window where a drift of silt has recently formed a small improvisational spiral jetty. The water curls around it. What was once a wooded hillside above the opposite bank is now an open meadow with a handful of saplings. She pauses. "Things are always changing," she says. "When we first came up here from the city, it was always the white noise of the waterfall. It was dramatic, powerful, incredible to look at, a spectacle to admire, but more than that, it was the sound. But now I feel more as though I am *in* nature. I can hear the birdcalls, the ducks." The water is a subdued, but no less powerful presence in their lives, and her affiliation with it now is closer, more as a participant than a spectator. With the dam in place and the water deeper years ago, the family had been able to paddle upstream for half a mile or so. Now they put on boots and waders and take walks up the streambed. "I like it better now," she says. When she notes quietly that her mother, despite her affection for the turmoil and rush of the old waterfall, would have been "okay with it too," I take it to be some generational family corollary that has come with reconnecting the upper and lower streams.

Her words about how we experience place remind me of the two landscapes we can occupy—one outside the self, the other within—that Barry Lopez writes about in his essay "Landscape and Narrative." The first is the one we see, weather, geology, plant and animal species, the shadows, the textures, the tracks, water, and light. "One learns a landscape finally not by knowing the name or identity of everything in it, but by perceiving the relationships in it—like that between the sparrow and the twig." The second landscape is interior, a set of like relationships, but between speculations, intuitions and formal ideas, some of these relationships obvious, other impenetrably subtle. What makes a place comprehensible, Lopez suggests, is the relationship between these: "The interior landscape responds to the character and subtlety of an exterior landscape: the shape of the individual mind is affected by the land as it is by genes."[5]

I revisit the stream later on a humid June morning in 2023. After a week of steady rain, the creek is muddy, running high and fast and full of sediment, and shore weeds, thickets of mugwort especially, run riot along the banks. The household garbage that once accumulated there is missing though, and Dan tells me in an email that "the volume of junk decreased dramatically two or three years after the dam was removed. I haven't pulled a toilet out of there in six years or so." Of interest now is finding out what *is* there. Earlier in the year, the Hudson River Estuary Program had initiated testing in the East Branch of the Wappinger Creek. Called "Monitoring Unassessed Stream Segments," the program aimed to collect information about the overall condition of those waterways flowing into the Hudson River that have limited water quality data. The results, to be shared with local partners, landowners, and watershed groups, will be put to use in planning and local land decisions and watershed management. Now I'm there to meet with Tom Niekrewicz, a water resource specialist at the estuary program and coordinator of the monitoring effort. Along with his assistant, Caleigh Millette, he plans on swinging by once a month from June to October for the next two years to get baseline data at this section of the creek.

Sitting on the stone steps leading down to the creek that Hilary and Dan had put in, I watched Tom and Caleigh do their assessment. Their testing has less to do with the dam removal, they told me; it's just a section of the creek where there isn't much data, so they were there to start collecting some. But if spending an hour of a June afternoon at the edge of the stream was informative, it was pure pleasure as well. I know it could take over a year to get the data analyzed, but it's good to know that the process has started.

Tom is tall, thin, bearded, and affable, and his efforts to answer my questions with limited arcane technical language seems more a product of his innate goodwill and hope to clarify the value of his work than of the belabored challenge of translation that scientists are sometimes called upon to practice when speaking with nonscientists. He grew up in Stone Ridge across the river, which makes him a local, and he has been doing this testing for three years. His background and training are broad. Before that, he was working for New York State Parks in Albany, helping out with sampling, filling in, working on permits, inventories of drinking systems, reviewing projects for environmental impact, a lot of different things. With tattoos on her upper arms that range from ferns and leaves to exquisite snails, Caleigh brings a sense of pleasure to her practice of rigorous measurements. Maybe it's just that it's an early summer day, but there is something in their enthusiasm for the work, their high boots and waders, chartreuse safety vests with orange stripes, blue gloves, and green DEC baseball caps that bring an almost festive element to the afternoon.

Caleigh wades into the stream to test for mercury, fills a sample jar with water, puts it in a plastic Ziploc bag, then wraps it in bubble wrap. Then she and Tom move on to something called a probe, an instrument with a watertight tubelike casing that contains the sensors, a handheld monitor and screen, and a cable connecting the two. The sensors will record data for temperature, pH, dissolved oxygen, conductivity, and salinity, and then transmit it digitally to the monitor. So as not to kick up sediment that might block the sensors, she wades upstream twenty feet or so and leaves the probe lying on the bed of the creek for the ten or fifteen minutes it will take to get the samples. Next up is an apparatus called a DH81 depth integrated sediment sampler. It measures amounts of trace metals, suspended sediments, bacteria levels if relevant, nutrients, and whatever other chemical and biological characteristics may distinguish a body of water. The equipment—a "churn" that looks like a white plastic bucket and a collection bottle with a pointed nozzle and long handle—has already been thoroughly cleaned, but Caleigh acclimates the equipment anyway, flushing out any vestiges that might remain from previous site visits. She repeats the process three times.

The sampler is designed to collect water from the entire water column. To avoid collecting silt and sediment, it never touches the bed of the stream, gathering water instead from the lower and upper water levels. That's more easily done in the center of the stream where the current is faster than close to the shore where there is suspended sediment. To get a representative sample, Caleigh dips the collection bottle once close to the streambed and again close to the surface. She gets five samples, one in the middle of the stream, two on the left, and two on the right to get a good cross section. The nozzle captures water at a slower rate than if she just stuck the whole bottle in. As she's doing this, Tom is filling out a survey itemizing the physical characteristics of the stream and taking photographs upstream and downstream. Extra information, he calls it. Then they take the water in the churn bucket and distribute it into ten sample jars in the truck. They'll be back in a month to run another batch of tests. A groundhog on the other side of the stream is watching us intently. A cabbage moth flutters by.

Earlier in the week, I had read an article in the newspaper about geophysicists paying renewed attention to slight variations in the spin of the planet. They were learning that such subtle deviations, known as "polar motion," could be the result of the distribution—and redistribution—of water caused by such factors as excessive groundwater extraction, changes in moisture in the soil, melting glaciers, vanishing icesheets—and impoundments in reservoirs. Added up, it seems, such shifts in the weight of water can cause the axis of the earth to drift, just ever so slightly.[6] That the very centerline of the planet can be affected by such circumstances is pretty much beyond my fathoming. Yet on this summer afternoon as I watch Caleigh taking her samples and measurements, I wonder if paying attention to such small coordinates can help us to grasp those larger ones that seem almost too large to take in.

I meet up with Tom and Caleigh again when they return to the East Branch to sample for macroinvertebrates. It's eighty degrees, hot and humid, and after a strong rain earlier in the week the creek has branched, pooled, formed a new section of strong riffles, then a quiet eddy, reconfigured yet again. The gravel beds and little island have taken new shapes, and day lilies are blooming on the banks. The macros are tiny organisms without backbones, aquatic insects, snails, and crayfish in nymph and larval stages. As well as providing food for reptiles, birds, fish, and amphibians, they consume live organic material. These small ambassadors of water quality from the streambed observe their own hierarchy: water pennys, stonefly nymphs, and caddisfly larva are all evidence of good water quality; damselfly nymphs, dragonfly nymphs, and crayfish can withstand some water pollution; and leeches, midge larva, and rat-tailed maggots can tolerate more polluted water. It's all information that will help in permitting, water management, and land-use planning.

Tom and Caleigh run more water quality tests just as they did a month earlier, but Tom is already on the alert for the critters. As he scrolls through the information appearing from the probe, he's also thigh deep in the stream, itemizing what he sees: a minnow, I hear him say, and moments later, a crayfish. His tone of enthusiasm falters only slightly when he spots a water snake, but the reptile slips off before he can identify the species.

The macroinvertebrates' preferred habitat is near more shallow and riffled areas, and when Tom and Caleigh start to wade fifty feet upstream to just such a spot, I can't help but follow them. I am without waders and boots, the water midstream where we step in is well over my knees, and I am alarmingly aware now that it is home territory to a water snake. But it is still an easy call: my pants are fast drying, I don't want to miss a minute of what they are doing, and stream walking on a July afternoon is pure pleasure. It's a little slippery. I remember hearing that before the removal project, you could sink into the silt in this area for fifteen or eighteen inches. That silt is long gone now, replaced by the larger rocks and cobble of the substrate. As my legs become immersed in the drift of the cool current, my steps slow and my balance on the rocky creek bed adjusts. Only slightly euphoric, I feel that my material being has temporarily gone from being solid to simply becoming another component of this fluid stream.

The sampling equipment is simple: the kick net, a square mesh net with a pole handle used to collect aquatic macroinvertebrates; a shallow tray in which to put the sample so they can sift through it; a sieve; and a sample jar. As Tom heads into the middle of the stream to start sampling,

Caleigh settles on the shore to work on the survey for the riparian area. The survey questions include bank stability, scouring, and erosion; cover, meaning the logs, rocks, trees, fallen branches, and other places that offer habitat; incision of stream, the amount of sand and sediment around the rocks on the bed of the creek. They also check the flow status. The channel is full from earlier rains: ten on a scale of zero to twenty.

As Caleigh sits on the bank, completing the survey, Tom works with the kick net to get the samples for macroinvertebrate samples. He positions the net to face upstream, then stands in front of it and kicks up the rocks on the bed, stirring up the gravel, sand, bugs, and macroinvertebrates that all end up in the collection net. As in water sampling, he repeats this five times: Once in the middle, twice on the left, and twice on the right. After a few minutes, he pours the collection of rocks, sand, sediment, and, with any luck, macroinvertebrates into the tray, and he and Caleigh sit on a grassy area on the bank to see what they've got. Caleigh gently pokes through it with a stick, Tom with a stalk of long grass. They add some creek water. They're watching closely. It'll take a few minutes for the sample to settle and for the critters to show themselves. Then even I can see that it has come alive with tiny creatures amidst the bits of shale, stone, and creek water that catch the light. Tom stirs up the sample just a bit, and the two of them quietly catalogue what they see: a water penny, mayfly, crayfish, a worm, a Dobson fly maybe, possibly a caddisfly. Perhaps, too, larva from dragonflies and damselflies. They examine the larger rocks for any bits of life that may be affixed to them, then get rid of the rocks. "There are probably a lot of species here we're not seeing," Tom says quietly. The lab will document everything more completely and precisely later.

In arguments about dam removal, the waterways in which obsolete dams have been removed are sometimes called "retired rivers." No longer serving industry and commerce, they are thought to be without purpose. On this summer afternoon, though, this creek is nothing like that. If anything, its momentum has picked up, and its regeneration of stream life signals renewal and energy. Watching Tom and Caleigh sift through the sand and stones is akin to witnessing some mission nearly biblical in nature, that universal human impulse to search out the good, whether it is winnowing wheat from chaff, separating molten metal from dross, or extracting flecks of gold from soil aggregates. Here, the prizes are bugs and worms, tiny spots and speckles of biodiversity. It's slow work, and it's mesmerizing. "I could do this all day," Caleigh says softly, mostly to herself, and I believe her because I could too. I think how naturally it sometimes comes to us to pay attention, to disappear into that miniature world, one that is hardly visible, barely in our understanding, yet one that captures our imagination. That we have this innate curiosity and ability gives me hope.

Caleigh puts as much of the material that will fit into the sample jar, leaving only a couple of inches at the top. She's removed the larger pieces of shale and rock, tossing them into the creek, then dumps the rest of the sample back into the creek, saying "You can't keep everything." The lab will find what their eyes have missed. Back at the truck they fill the remainder of the jar with ethanol. Though killing them in the process, it'll preserve the critters. But, they rationalize, it's for science, and they pack up the samples in coolers to ship them overnight to the lab.

I routinely vow to spend less time looking at screens, yet I've fallen into a habit I can't quite help: checking into the loop function on my iPhone to watch this creek flow. I know the loop of the running stream is an artificial gimmick on my little device. I know it is not continuity but repetition, after only a few seconds, some techno-facsimile of continuity. I know that continuity and repetition operate on different principles and reside in separate universes. I know there is nothing here to suggest the ever-changing character of a stream bed. I know all this, but still. In my kitchen at breakfast or at my desk on a wintry day, there is something about tapping the little picture on the screen, watching it come to life, and staring at this endless loop of green creek streaming with riffles over rock that brings pure pleasure. This dumb little video does its quiet and sure work on my brain.

But then, of course, there is something real in the loop after all. Sometimes there *is* a circularity to human experience. Sometimes things *do* repeat themselves incessantly without changing at all—the same riffle of water, the same gray rock, the same gust of wind blowing the same leaf, over and over and over. The little stream on repeat gets it perfectly. And I have to wonder which of these circumstances is more true to life. Both are useful frameworks. This is the kind of thinking you arrive at when looking at water of any kind. It does not surprise me to learn later that Hilary has also taken to checking in on the stream remotely. She has installed a webcam near the stream and from her home in Brooklyn can watch the changes in the water level as the seasons and storms come and go, the rippling of the water, the birds overhead. She can also see the weeping willow tree planted with her mother's ashes across the stream, its leaves blowing in the breeze. "There is something soothing about the timeless continuity," Hilary writes me in an email.

We have so many ways of measuring time. Perhaps because we find geological time and our place in the 4.6 billion year continuum of earth's existence incomprehensible, we have devised multiple other measurements for that deep time, among them divine, human, psychological, and civic. In recent years, that curious phrase *in real time* has also entered common usage. First used in the computer industry to describe the immediacy with which data is processed, instantly and as it is received, the words are used now to distinguish what happens in the moment from what occurs through delays of the digital realm, in time lags and recordings, and through the lapses of social media postings. It seems strange that things happening in the moment need to be specified as such; the word *now* has always worked pretty well. My own personal theory is that whatever *real time* happens to be, our ideas about it and how we experience it are derived from the landscape; and that we arrive at some understanding of our place in the grand continuum through features of the natural world—mountains, sky, rocks, water, and the way space is arranged around them. Watching streaming water brings us to a different sense of time than seeing the stars scattered across a night sky or viewing a mountain or far horizon

Distance, space, height, light, stillness, and motion, in elusive and ineffable combinations, help us to form our understanding of the scale of time. I know that Einstein believed that time on earth and time in space pass at different speeds, and that changeability in gravitational pull allows time to pass more quickly at higher altitudes. I can't speak to that, but it's enough for me to know that water, too, allows time to pass at varying rates. Jonathon Keats, an artist who uses water as a measure of time, has devised an instrument to calculate these variants. His "River Clock," a digital display illuminated on the façade of the Anchorage Museum in Alaska, calibrates time using the flow of five rivers and streams and their historical changes. Data from these waterways provided by the United States Geological Survey (USGS) are averaged out to reflect the shifts caused by drought, rainfall, snowmelt, and other conditions affected by climate change; river time picks up when the current flow is faster than the historical average but slows when the flow falls below it. Keats's river clock suggests that Alaska mean river time is changeable, unpredictable, and without the regularity of standardized atomic time; and that monitoring these fluctuations is a way of paying greater attention to ground conditions.

In my own personal system of mathematics, I also often look to river time—not a methodical or quantifiable practice of calculation nor one that includes flow data from the USGS. Yet it remains a meaningful way to arrange the gauge of time, one that captures its alternating speed and stillness. Water speaks to time standing still and time racing away from us. Perhaps we have an intuitive grasp of both its immobility and its swiftness because we recognize in it the shine, the quick glimmer, the obscure depth of our own mortality. Scientists have their own reasons for calling streams "dynamic systems," but for me it's about their capacity for speed and stasis alike, both components of real time as I understand it to be.

~

Restorative landscape design of the twenty-first century tends to be a hybrid affair. I take in the saplings, the reconfigured channel, the new shrubs stabilizing the banks and know that all of these look to an earlier landscape for their cues. But it is impossible to replicate earlier conditions—the weather is warmer now, wetter too, winter arrives later in the year, spring just a bit earlier, and the storms are more intense. Certain species of trees and shrubs have vanished entirely, while others have arrived. All of which suggest that the word *restoration* may be more aspirational than accurate. But that said, the creek has been restored to its original path. This little stretch follows its original course without ambiguity.

I think again of the biologists taking measure of the new fish migration and the difficulty in taking such calculations. While water quality and sediment load may be quantifiable and easy to count, test, and assess, other factors are more difficult to gauge. Dam removal may advance fish passage, but data on the migration of eels, herring, and resident fish can be elusive. Their journey happens underwater. The fish are submerged. Their passage remains largely invisible, and as a visual species, we humans tend to respond to things we see and experience directly. We see the birds outside the feeder at the kitchen window, and the path of waterbirds is visible to us, as are the wheeling of the gulls and the more direct path of the blue heron. But when something unseen vanishes, that's a little abstract, and our response can be muted. Electrofishing can determine abundance and density, but such data collection is something few of us practice. Most of us have little direct experience with the presence and absence of fish. As John Waldman told me, "If you had these giant walls on land and birds were smashing into them, people would freak. But because this happens in water, you don't see it."[7]

Invisible travel corridors and unmarked pathways can be found across earth and water everywhere. At a college where I once taught, a student mapped the desire paths of the entire campus, those scuffed footpaths made across grass, between buildings, through fields and woods, those shortcuts and improvisational routes not formulated by landscape architects but nonetheless apparent through constant use. And for years, I slowed down when driving and approaching a sharp turn on a country road near our house. I knew from experience that animals often crossed the road here, had seen deer, wild turkeys, even the occasional bear. Later, in preparing our town's Natural Resources Inventory, I found that much of the woodland adjacent to that country road had been broken up into patches, fragmented by development. Yet core forest on both sides of this particular bend made it part of a passageway for wildlife. It is likely that all of us have these unmarked streets and avenues, ones that go unnamed and usually unnoticed, outside of established travel corridors, yet imprinted all the same in our own archive of cognitive maps. Aboriginal people in Australia observe songlines in their travel, an oral recitation cataloguing phenomenon of the natural landscape—waterways, stone formations, particular trees—all vital navigational information passed on through generations, a system of signals to be used by travelers finding their way across unfamiliar topography.

Unseen travel paths make me wonder if eels have made it this far upstream. None have turned up in the surveys, but that doesn't mean they're not present. Throughout the watershed they've been found by fisherman in headwaters where they are little expected. Fran Dunwell had told me about strong documentary evidence for eels' ability to travel upstream: For each dam blocking the movement of eels, about ten percent of eels are unable to get over that barrier. Yet eels have an amazing ability to get over a dam, even up and over a waterfall. "It became apparent to us," Dunwell said, "that removing a second barrier, a third barrier, fourth barrier, fifth barrier, would benefit eels. It wouldn't benefit them as much as removing the first barrier, but every barrier along the way would be progress for eels to find habitat where they can mature. And they need to spread out."

I am not surprised, then, to get Tom's email telling me that "Based off this location and the barriers downstream of the East Branch Wappinger Creek and Wappinger Creek it would make it challenging for eels to travel upstream to this site, but not impossible. If there are any eels it's likely one large female eel." I find myself confronted yet again with this inevitable fact of ecological appraisal: The natural world is as full of the immeasurable as it is of the measurable, especially when running water is involved. Certainly any such evaluation we make in this time of environmental losses must account for both what we can calculate and what we cannot. The water slipping over the stones, the light spilling over the water, the glint of a fish, all of these fleeting occurrences remind us of what we can track and what we can't.

A few weeks later, Hilary emails me to ask if I know anything about a bright yellow dot that has appeared on a rock on the opposite bank. Is the new marker some sudden sign of vandalism or is it some significant marker for water level used by a scientist? Both of these seem improbable, but either way, a reminder of inescapable human impact. As it turns out, the dot was a reblaze of a marker made in 2017 on a remnant of the old dam face, used as a benchmark for surveying data upstream and downstream. It is on a bit of shale and scrapes off easily. Still, it seems like a little souvenir of the inevitable traces we leave of ourselves, even when we are simply watching to see what happens.

I first visited the site in early 2021, during the Covid-19 pandemic. Hilary, Dan, and I stayed outdoors, masked, as they took me to the creek, showed me the abutments, and told me about what it had taken to dismantle the dam. Over the next couple of years we have come to know each other better, and in the summer of 2023, my husband and I join them for dinner in the millhouse with other mutual friends from our college days. The days of wearing facemasks have gone, and over a glass of wine and perfectly seared tuna, I learn that the coincidences of our college years are greater than either of us had imagined: At different times during the late seventies, Hilary and I had both occupied the same room in an old farmhouse serving as an off-campus dorm. I know that there is a science to coincidence. Those unexpected and inexplicable alliances of people, events, and dates that seem to lie outside of simple cause and effect are perceived as random by many. To others, their patterns suggest a possible order to a disordered world.

Carl Jung believed that coincidences, defying our assumptions about probability, were signals of an underlying accord in experience and perception, and that such invisible connections, or what he called "synchronicities," were key to human understanding and behavior. I can't quite bring myself to believe in such certainties, yet know that if I assign significance to coincidences, it is because they offer a way to think through the meaning of ordinary events—all the more so if water is the conduit for the connection. Throughout the evening, the backdrop to our conversation is the sound of high water rushing in the stream just outside the window.

Weirdly, perhaps, I suddenly find it easy to draw a connection between the millpond in its original state and the stream now. Until the 1850s, the creek was the site for flour, grist, plaster, and saw mills, and the hamlet of Hibernia today still has the intimate scale of its early days. Small historic houses remain nestled into the banks of the creek. Their siding may be composite or vinyl instead of wood clapboard, and a dumpster, a couple of outdoor grills, a steel Tuff Shed, and a few decorative house flags hanging on porches speak to the present moment. Yet the scale and closeness of the neighborhood easily evoke the thriving business hub that was once here. In an article published in a yearbook published in 1986 by the Dutchess County Historical Society, the writer imagines an early resident revisiting the hamlet 200 years after "it was carved out of the wilderness to serve its neighbors." He continues: "Surely the black cover on the dirt road he had once traveled would surprise him, but the road itself, its intersection, its sharp turns, the bridge, the mill dam and a number of the structures in the hamlet would be quite familiar . . . change in Hibernia has been gentle." He notes, too, that such hamlets emerged gradually, "frequently as a result of services complementary to a central enterprise, usually a mill," and that such businesses were central to the survival of the farm community.[8]

If it was then a community of shared support and goodwill, that sense of neighborly dependence may be a thing of the past. Not all the hamlet's current residents live there full-time, and of those who do, most work miles away. Still, I wonder if the collaborative effort it took to restore and reconnect this stream could be some contemporary iteration of that earlier community: defined not by geography but by shared objectives; determined not by place but by some clear constellation of sympathies, interests, and beliefs. Certainly this broad alliance between private landowners, engineers, local community, NYSDEC, and other regulatory agencies was a confluence of intent and effort that reflected the ethos of connectivity at the heart of the enterprise itself. And in serving as a template for a restored waterway, the old millhouse, its dismantled dam, and the flowing stream have continued to provide services complementary to a central enterprise.

Figure 5. Tidal backwater near where the Jamawissa Creek flows into the Hudson River.

Beauty Reconsidered

Jamawissa Creek

> I think we need to mix the concept of restoration with a little bit of John Lennon's "Imagine."
>
> —Laura Wildman

A small island with a bluff overlooks the confluence of the Jamawissa Creek and the Hudson River. The convergence of waterways has always engaged the human imagination, and today the wide mouth of the stream is a brackish tidal backwater, moving so quietly as to appear almost still before it flows under the railroad tracks and out into the river. It is framed by meadows of phragmites, the feathery heads of the weeds catching strands of sunlight, before becoming something else entirely as it converges with the vast and inexorable flow of the Hudson. Everything changes then—the movement of the water from languid to powerful; its color from a cloudy green to a silver shine; the smooth silk of the backwater to the scalloped surface of the river. The area has been cited by archeologists as a possible site for precontact burials, and it's not hard to understand why such a place might evoke a continuity of spirit. Any place where two waterways meet invariably suggests both a beginning and an end.

The riverfront is also a traditional place of community and enterprise. Before the arrival of Europeans, Native Americans used the river, streams, and adjacent lands here for fishing and seasonal hunting and gathering. Villages, some only temporary, had long been established along the riverbank for farming, until the arrival of Henry Hudson in 1609. The Dutch colonists who followed shifted land use to more conventional agriculture. By the nineteenth century, industrial brickmaking enterprises had also been founded near the river. A railroad was built along the shore of the river around 1850, making the area accessible to urban visitors, and by the end of that century, a hotel and a number of residences had been built on the island and adjacent areas. By the early twentieth century, though, the land was largely owned by a single family. What ultimately became known as the McAndrews estate was a working farm with a degree of Gilded Age elegance, including a manor house, several smaller residences, barns, and a cast-iron garden fountain. The splendor was short lived. By mid-century, the agricultural efforts were failing, taxes went unpaid, and the property fell into disrepair. Westchester County took ownership of the estate in the mid-sixties, demolishing most of the buildings. The land eventually became a public park, wooded and threaded with walking trails.[1]

Today, it is all part of Oscawana Park and Nature Preserve in Cortlandt, New York. Oak, maple, hickory, and ironwood make up that woodland, but vestiges of its earlier extravagant era remain scattered throughout—the foundations of the old manor house, stone walls and terraces, steps, pillars, remnants of an old stone chicken coop, the walls of a stone barn, an icehouse, and somewhat spectacularly, the barely discernible oval path of an old racetrack and crumbling iron fencing around it. Another remnant, of course, is the dam, along with the black-green muck of the impoundment behind it. A substantial concrete structure twenty-five feet high and 160 feet long, it had been built in the 1880s to create a reflecting pool, a convention of such estates at the time. Situated at a narrow area of the stream, a place where there is a substantial grade change, its purpose was largely aesthetic.

I first visit the site on an early May morning in 2022, when only a few trees have leafed out. The understory of the forest floor is only beginning to emerge—tiny white ephemerals, ferns, garlic mustard, a few spangles of early forsythia, sprigs of multiflora rosa. Although I can barely make out the shine of the river less than a mile away, I can sense it. This is a first barrier dam, the one on this tributary that is closest to the river, and its proximity to the Hudson gives its removal a different sense of urgency, an immediacy. Unlike those barriers many miles upstream with which I am more familiar, this one has a different presence: Knock a few of its stones away, disassemble the concrete, notch it down, and it is indeed a gateway to the Hudson; that grand highway to the ocean is nearly three miles wide here, and allowing the tributary to flow unobstructed into the river has an intuitive logic.

I am here to meet Suzette Lopane, a landscape architect with the Westchester County Department of Planning, so I can learn the site while following her as she works on tree identification. Part of the county's planning process for dam removal will be to determine the number of trees to bring down. The northern bank above the dam, though adjacent to an existing road, is too steep to allow for construction equipment, so woodlands to the south will have to be cleared for a twelve-foot-wide access road. Add to that the necessary areas for spoil pits for the sediment that will be removed from the pond, and a good deal of land is going to be disturbed. This means a lot of tree removal.

We parked down near the river, but before we even head up to the dam site, Lopane points out a sandbar that is visible at low tide, the stream being tidal up to the dam. She gestures to the rocks on the creek bed that signal a sediment deficit. Twenty years' worth of sediment, maybe some 30,000 cubic yards of it, could be released by the dam removal, she tells me. This is when I begin to fully grasp that removing and relocating that sediment is as much a part of the job as deconstructing the dam itself.

In her early fifties, Suzette has an open face, long curly hair, and a quick laugh. She has an easy manner, but when she is asked a question about, say, the funding for this project, or the number of trees that may have to be removed from the site, or the amount of sediment that will have to be removed, a stillness settles over her. Her eyes narrow, and her face doesn't quite harden, but you can see she is focusing on a subject that goes deep with her. What matters requires concentration, and that's what she gives it. As we are walking around an old path on the McAndrews estate framed by decorative metal fencing, she's thinking aloud. It's either iron or steel, she says. Iron ore was mined in the area. "When was steel forged?" she asks herself. "If I knew, I could date this." It's an innate curiosity and a way of challenging and questioning herself about what's around her, integral to the way she works. She grew up in New York, New Jersey, Tennessee, New Jersey again, then Texas, then attended Cornell University, and I suspect that all that moving around is what taught her to read landscape with such care.

We continue up the trail through a forest of red maples, Norway maples, sugar maples, oaks, tulip trees, black locust, beech, a few birch, and some ash, a number of these last infected and dying from the recent arrival of the emerald ash borer. I wonder if the few flowering dogwoods are remnants from old estate, but Lopane is more interested in the proliferation of Norway maples, a nonnative species. With a distinctive fine patterning on their bark, they flower and leaf in earlier than other maple species, which makes them easy to spot today. And, casting early shade on the forest floor, they make it difficult for native plants and early ephemerals to grow there, thus diminishing the health of the forest's understory. Bringing them down is not going to degrade the site, and could, in fact, be for the best. How convenient it would be if tree removal could be limited to this species.

Now, every few steps, she looks at her map. Deer browse has thinned out the woods, there is little understory, the tree canopy is disparate, and the paths we take don't always seem to conform to what the surveyor has charted. "That's always the way it is," Lopane grumbles. She has marked a lot of trees in yellow to help with wayfinding, "to figure out where the hell he was." In theory, I'm drawn to the idea of working with a map that simply offers a diagram of trees—*follow the way of the trees* has a nice primal ring to it, and just the facts of the forest, the path, and the map form a triad with mythological overtones across time and culture. Navigating the twisting trail through looming branches, shifting shadows, and birdsong overhead is a parable for the human quest for meaning, and for Carl Jung, the forest represented the unconscious. But on this particular morning, my tireless efforts to search out the epic in the everyday are becoming problematic. A twinned tulip tree seems to be marked on the map as an oak, and along with the abundance of nonnative species, diseased trees, spoil pits, and bits of rusting industrial detritus, the exercise seems like a twenty-first century parody of the timeless human endeavor. Wayfinding with a map of trees? "It's a horrible idea," Lopane says. "We shouldn't have to do it." We come across some old tires that have been dumped in the woods. "I wish he'd put these on the map," she mutters.

Lopane marks the Norway maples on her map in orange and we continue down to what she hopes will serve as the spoils area to contain the sediment taken from the pond. Several unnaturally large chasms in the ground near the dam, known as "borrow pits," are evidence of areas in which soil was removed for use elsewhere. Their original purpose here remains unknown. Was the earth here dug up to help form the racetrack? Or was there a brick operation for building construction in New York City? It is possible, too, that the soil was used to help construct the dam itself, possibly an earthen interior with masonry face. The layers and layers of history here, though, remain a mystery. Skunk cabbage is flourishing in one of the crevasses close to the dam, raising the question of whether it is part of a wetland. Which then raises the next question of whether NYSDEC will allow it to serve as an area for dredged sediment. We stand next to a huge tulip tree near the first possible spoils pit. "You and I would be under the fill," Lopane says matter-of-factly. "The tulip tree is unlikely to survive. I'm not going to worry about it."

The impoundment, decades removed from its origins as a serene reflecting pool, is now a vast pool of sludge. I look at what seems to be a gargantuan gulley that might be designated to hold the sediment and, knowing absolutely nothing, I tell her it seems like way more space than is needed. She waves the map in front of me, showing me the vast sweep of blue that represents the stream and its impoundment. "There's at least nine feet of sediment here," she says. "The aerials don't capture this. You can't Google this. You need to have boots on the ground." Not for the first time, I realize how difficult it is to fully grasp the scale of physical space. Suzette pauses to orient herself again with the trees. Attuned to the miniscule as well as to the gargantuan, she exclaims with delight at a tiny gray and white bird. "A nuthatch!"

We've found ourselves on a path that is indicated nowhere on the tree map. The path lies between two potential dredge areas so perhaps it could serve as an access road? Maybe. That's only the first question. We are still nowhere close to a count of how many trees will have to come down and subsequently be replaced. In suburban areas, Lopane tells me, you can use caliper measurements for the thickness, or diameter, of the trunks of the downed trees to determine how best to replace them. That makes less sense in a forest. Do you plant the same species of trees? If so, at what age? And if most of the trees coming down are Norway maples, undesirable to begin with, how do you even think about replacing them? Do the components of forest diversity today bear any resemblance to what they were half a century ago? Black locusts, common today in woodlands of the Northeast, are not native to the area and can spread quickly and aggressively. And shorter, milder winters will affect the various species of maple trees that have long flourished here. Most of us come to understand at some point in our lives that measuring what has been lost is never a simple process, and replacing what has been lost can be impossible. It is much the same in forest ecology. There are no equivalencies that quite make sense. Besides, there is no standard period for what is considered *the past*, no ideal time to return to. To some it means the 1930s, for others, the 1780s. The term is arbitrary and usually refers to the period after the arrival of Europeans, a perspective that doesn't help much either.

The questions take me back to a conversation I had with Laura Wildman, who shared her own doubts about how far restorative efforts could go. Even aggressive invasive species management and native planting, she told me, won't necessarily prevent nonnative species from returning and dominating a disturbed area:

> Ecological restoration can't solve our greater invasive species problem. It's in the seed bank. But what's also in that seedbank are historic native species. You can work as hard as you can to do some management on it, but it's not going to solve the problem. These waves of nonnative species and the rigor with which they take over can't be solved by little patchworks of doing something here, doing something there. This is an issue on a much larger ecological scale.

Advocating for a degree of acceptance, Wildman said, "You just have to understand at what time period you are taking this dam out. You're not taking this dam out a hundred years ago. You're taking this dam out now. And right now we have problems with sewage, with stormwater runoff, with invasive species. These restoration projects aren't going to solve all that. It's the reality of what the environment we are working in now is." She has come to define *restoration* as having to do with restoring natural processes, creating something self-sustaining:

> It should be able to be here whether we are or not. We should be able to vanish. Restoration of a natural system should restore natural function and process. There shouldn't be maintenance involved. But I've designed projects that require maintenance. And you know why? Because there may be a building right there. Or there may be a railroad right there. And we are trying to maintain them. But let's try to be clear about what we're doing. That's the protection of the infrastructure part. The restoration part should be restoration of natural function.

That restoration is tricky is not news to me. Even the words we use reflect confusion. Jamawissa, meaning "place of the small beaver," is the Native name for this stream, though it has also been called the "Old Mill Stream," and since the early eighteenth century has been more commonly known as "Furnace Brook." Yet "Jamawissa" is the name often used now by those working on the site, and Lopane tells me about her own pleasure at seeing the stream identified this way in an old map she's come across. Although I have taken to using that name myself, in part to avoid confusion with Furnace Pond, fifty miles to the north, I still have trouble believing that language can genuinely serve as a restorative tactic. I have no doubt that how we communicate reflects cultural myths and historical biases and have always wanted to believe that the careful use of words can affect thought and behavior. Perhaps there is something innate in us that wants to honor the past, to return to it, relive it if we could, correct our errors, do *right*. It is human to want to start over, have another chance, plant the right tree, use the old word. Land acknowledgment is principled and well intentioned. Yet I am just as certain that changing the name of a place rarely corresponds to changing its value or its use and often find it suspect to assume that simply using a Native name confers respect.

By now it's the end of the afternoon. Before we head home, Lopane tells me to check out the oyster shells near the riverbed at low tide. Even today signs of eroded middens, refuse piles of oyster shells, some dating from 7,000 years ago, continue to be found in the estuary. Oysters need a considerable level of salt to thrive, and their flourishing depended on the degree of salinity brought in by the tide. Over the passage of centuries, the proliferation of oyster beds came and went with varying levels of salinity, all of it nonetheless testimony to the harvesting traditions practiced by Native Americans. Following the arrival of Europeans in the seventeenth century, the hydrology of the river was irrevocably transformed: Over subsequent generations forests were logged, streams channelized and dammed, the railroad constructed, dykes built, sediment dredged, wetlands eliminated, and much of the shoreline hardened, all land use choices that reduced biodiversity and diminished salinity levels. Along with overharvesting, these gradually obliterated the oyster beds.

Because the stream's proximity to the Hudson River has rendered it a sensitive area with historical significance, the county requisitioned an archaeological survey before any plans for dam removal and sediment disposal could even be considered. Shovel tests at the area immediately around the dam, much of it sloping and steep, with rock outcrops and tidal marshes alike, turned up no signs of precontact presence, but on more level areas and especially those areas close to the river, there were indications of burial sites and other precontact habitation. Naturalist John Phillips, a local long familiar with both the ecology and archeology of the site and who contributed to the survey notes that "The closer you get to the river, the more sensitive sites you find, oyster middens, stone tools. At the mouth of the creek, they were probably catching eels and herring."[7]

The oyster shells are nothing but remnants in the muck of the riverbed now, but they still work to remind me that this streamscape lives on a far broader timetable than anything I can easily imagine. After my first visit, I've made it a habit to walk down to the river, to stand alongside its wide gray sheen, to imprint again in my mind this place where the stream meets the river, and to remind myself that restoration is not about a particular time period, nor even necessarily about ecological balance. It would be absurd to think that the changes in the river's shoreline or hydrology at large could be reversed. As ambiguous as it may be, the idea that it is about process makes the most sense of all.

Over the course of the following year, I visit the site with Lopane from time to time. Permitting—from NYSDEC, the Army Corps of Engineers, and the Town of Cortlandt—is going slowly; not unexpected, but still frustrating. In midwinter 2023, I join a diverse group of naturalists, educators, community science volunteers, and activists all gathered to exchange notes and gain familiarity both with the site and the challenges posed by removing dam. And to learn more about the beneficial impact of removing man-made dams before work begins—why dams are installed, removed, and what the results will be. Suzette is there along with George Jackman, David DeLucia, director of parks facilities for Westchester County, John Phillips, and an assortment of other educators and volunteers. It's a sunny day in the fifties, warm for February, and the wide mouth of the stream before it goes under the tracks and out into the river is cloudy, gray, brackish. It feels like a spring day, but it's not. A bald eagle floats by overhead as we are waiting in the parking lot. Indian Point, the nuclear plant shuttered in 2021, is just a few miles upriver. Along with the barrier coming down and the burgeoning population of eagles after near extinction only a few decades ago, the raptor overhead reads as an auspicious symbol of the area's continuing restoration.

My reverie is cut short by more pragmatic observations of the site as we head upstream. The remnants of an old brick pumphouse near the lower stream are covered in moss and graffiti; along with piping leading uphill, it has led to conjecture that the pond provided water for the estate, its manor house, outbuildings, barns, and fountain, along with an extensive underground water and sewage system. Phillips tells me his educated guess is that the pond was built to supply water to the house, stables, barns, and outbuildings. It's a pretty big dam, he says, and speculates it's probably too high for a purely ornamental reflecting pond. Other remnants of old piping laid parallel to the stream suggest water may also have been carried to the railroad tracks running alongside the Hudson River. Possibly the water was used for the coal-fired steam engines used at that time that needed water to drive the wheels. The wondering tone of our conversation about the past is punctuated by present reality, a moment at once both base and radiant: We step across a fallen log, encrusted with moss and splotched with scat, but it's spangled with iridescent fish scales that could just possibly signal the return of otters. Jackman and Phillips are beaming.

The Jamawissa dam had become a first barrier dam only recently. In November 2020, a smaller, five-foot-high, seventy-five-foot-long fieldstone dam closer to the river had been dismantled. Its removal was an example of what Laura Wildman calls a less-is-more approach, which essentially allows the river to do the work. In this case, a tractor outfitted with a concrete breaker had taken down in a single day a structure that had been there for a century. With low costs, nothing structural added, and without requiring maintenance, this relatively passive approach allows the waterway to restore itself. And it is one that can be used when there are no sensitive habitats, no impact on infrastructure, and no potential for increased flooding, when sediment is uncontaminated and can be washed downstream without causing harm.[3]

White suckers, a freshwater species, were spotted swimming upstream almost immediately. Blue crabs followed, along with brown trout, eels, and herring. Stone masonry from the dam's spillway was used to reinforce the new channel, and a year later, trees and shrubs were planted to stabilize the bank and provide shade to create a cooler habitat. With the stream beginning to move and sediment naturally redistributing, a stagnant backwater again became a free-flowing and dynamic waterway. It may have been a small project, but as Jackman said at the time, it's a form of liberation: "Removing a dam, it's not just for yourself or the creek, but for all the organisms. And you've opened up the habitat and you've created these riparian corridors. You get to change the world."[4]

Changing the world upstream would demand more planning and engineering. In some such projects, the channel is locked in place and there is an emphasis on stabilization. Restoration infrastructure may be required by regulators, and ongoing maintenance may be needed as well. Costs are also higher than in the more passive approach. Conventional dam removal, especially for smaller structures, diverts the water away from the site with a system of siphons and pumps, then takes down the dam in dry conditions. Here, a different strategy is in place. The upper Jamawissa dam is a Class A barrier: There are no residences downstream, and a small bridge spanning the lower creek is the only real infrastructure. The plan is to notch the dam, taking it down in four-foot sections to lower the water level by increments, to remove and resettle the sediment, and allow the stream to find its way. Ninety days might pass between section removals, and it may take over a year to complete. Abutments will likely remain in place, and the banks of the brook kept as intact as possible.

Notching down the dam in increments leaves time to learn what that sediment does. Some of it will be deposited in spoils areas on the site, while much of it will be permitted to flow downstream. Will the banks be reconfigured? What about all the cobble there now, those stream rocks rounded by age and abrasion? Will new sandbars be formed? What will the mix of fine sediment and cobble be? Where will the center of the channel be? There are no answers. Once the dam is notched, you'll see where the river wants to go, Lopane says. There are two possibilities here. Either engineer an artificial channel or let the stream find its own channel. What you don't want is an entrenched stream. "You don't want the stream banks to be steep if the longitudinal pitch is flat because that would mean the stream isn't connected to its floodplain."

Princeton Hydro in Trenton, New Jersey, is the engineering firm overseeing the deconstruction, and part of the job is predicting the flow of sediment and the course the channel will eventually take. When I speak with Geoffrey Goll, president of the company, he tells me that anticipating stream flow is a process of both imagining the past and anticipating the future:

> When you are looking to design a dam removal, it's not like looking at a building or a field where you might do some grading or construction. You're not able to directly and visually see and touch the landscape that you're going to be working with when the dam is removed. You don't know what the history of the dam was. You don't know what the history of the floodplain was. A river may have had a wide floodplain naturally flowing before humans came around and started modifying the landscape. After they put the dam in, they could have filled in the floodplain and put a road in, they put utilities in. And so you have to try to use all the best information you can—you can go in with a probe and probe around, you use bathometric surveys, you're looking at historical maps, historical aerials, you're doing potentially borings in the impoundment.
>
> At the same time, though, you're also anticipating the future. If the dam was put in 150 years ago, and now we're having more intense rainfall, the flows are a lot higher now than

they were before. So it may not react the same way. But a lot of times, you will have an upstream reference where it is unimpounded. And so the stream has had a chance to re-establish or evolve into the current state of climate, but it is something you have to consider. And so it is really important to use the most updated precipitation data that you possible can. And even try to predict a little bit into the future. In New Jersey the flood hazard regulations have been revised so that you now don't only have to look at current rainfall. You also need to look at 2100. They want you to model that as well to determine where your floodplains are. And so we're learning slowly. But we're learning.

It's like a prediction, Goll concludes, one that takes in experience, education, and expertise to anticipate the course of the waterway without the dam. It's a design that tries to foresee known unknowns, unknown unknowns.

In our conversation, Laura Wildman had called river restoration "a form of expressionism, but instead of expressing your own vision of a river to evoke an emotional response, you are expressing the river's vision to evoke an ecological response. It's a philosophy suggesting that rivers could benefit from less physical manipulation, or tinkering, and a greater emphasis on long-term planning."[5] I remember how wary she is of the word *restoration*. The underlying premise to her work is that streams and streambanks are dynamic features. "Riffles move," she has said.

> Meanders move. Shorelines move. Beaches move. Forests migrate. Meadows change. None of this stuff is meant to have the kinds of artificial boundaries that we put on them because of property lines and everything else. I think we need to mix the concept of restoration with a little bit of John Lennon's "Imagine." To imagine, you know, there are no property lines. No state and federal borders. Imagine all that stuff that makes no sense in an ecological landscape.
>
> That's what I love about removing dams. You restore sediment transport processes. And the river can move there again. It can change. But you also have to remind the people you are doing the project for that it *will* change, that a tree will fall, that a bank will erode, that this will happen, because that's what natural rivers do. But when we are in an urban landscape

we are trying to reconnect people to a river, get access down to them . . . the idea of being able to allow it to be dynamic and natural is almost impossible.

I meet up again with Suzette at the Jamawissa where she is doing fieldwork in mid-March 2023. It's a cloudy, early spring day, and the temperature is in the low fifties. It had rained earlier in the morning and is now just a little overcast. The water at the impoundment is still, the buildup of nutrients resulting in stratification and eutrophication. So much sediment has accumulated behind the dam that there is barely any depth by the shore. The torpid character of the site seeps into the mood of the day, and it evokes Bachelard's musings on the melancholy that settles over him on the view to stagnant water. Being a French philosopher, he goes so far as to suggest that the view of dead water is "a daily tomb to everything that dies within us each day."[6]

Lopane isn't given to that kind of hyperbole, but her worries persist. She estimates that it will cost roughly $2.4 million to remove the dam. Comments about permitting are just coming in from NYSDEC, but her confidence wavers. Massive triple culverts just a half a mile upstream carry the stream under Route 9, a main county artery, and the water level there will drop after dam removal. How is fish passage going to happen there? What can be built for access? And only about a half mile or so upstream above the culverts is another dam; if the stretch between dams were longer, it might be easier to get funding. "That's the problem with the Northeast," Lopane says. "But you have to start somewhere." And the eel project is about to start, with the schoolkids gathering to monitor the glass eels on their annual migratory passage from the ocean up to the freshwater tributaries. Two migratory ducks are at the mouth of the stream. Returning to the parking lot through the woods, I see that the keystone in an arched doorway in one of the old stone ruins is engraved with *1907*, when the building was constructed. Suzette sees an early spring butterfly, a Mourning Cloak, as it is called.

She is a little more upbeat when I catch up with her on the phone in early June. Jim Tierney, Deputy Commissioner for Water Resources within NYSDEC, had recently given his support to the project, possibly because of the infrastructure bond act passed by the state. In 2022, voters in New York had approved a ballot proposition allocating $4.2 billion for environmental and community projects. The bond act allowed municipalities to access funding to protect water quality, address climate change, reduce pollution, create green jobs, and generally safeguard natural resources. As the supervisor for all water programs in the state, Tierney oversees dam safety, levees, and floodplain mapping and management. No surprise that Lopane is so enthusiastic about his support. "I was super, super happy to hear that," she says. "Sediment can be dirty, and his word has a lot of meaning."

Still, permitting is going slowly. The state requires that an archeological review be done for any work being done in a municipal park, and the permit from NYSDEC also asks for proof that such a report has been filed with the Department of Historic Preservation. But Lopane's presentation to the Westchester board of legislators about dam removal had been well received, and earlier in the week, the board had given its approval for funding. The county's five-year capital plan had included an appropriation setting aside $3 million in construction funding for the project once permits had been approved.

But I sense what is making Lopane especially happy is forward momentum on plantings for the site. In mid-June, I go back to Oscawana Park on a drizzly day to tag along as she reviews the area for plant and seed identification. She's been working with Lindsey Feinberg, a horticulturalist who has been collecting wild seeds, planting seeds, growing plants, and looking at indigenous ecotypes. Feinberg is a native plants curator at Hilltop Hanover Farm, a historic working farm and local environmental center focused on sustainable agriculture, stewardship and education. Lopane has recruited her to help specify what native plants might be brought in, whether as seeds or cultivated trees and shrubs. Areas that have been disturbed—whether through spoils deposits, drainage, or excavation—will need to be replanted. Just as the dam is going to be notched down gradually over a matter of months, so will vegetation be planted over time.

But what's going to work here? Suddenly the two women are speaking in a horticultural patois that I do my best to follow. Feinberg identifies some fowl manna grass, or *Glyceria striata*, a delicate native grass suited to shady wetlands and useful for erosion control, and Lopane suggests putting witch hazel on the list. It spreads around easily. Lopane's face falls, though, when she spots a beech tree in distress. She pulls me under a branch and shows me how the undersides of its leaves, viewed with the sunlight streaming through them, are marked with a pattern of dark striations. It's called interveinal banding and is a sign of Beech Leaf Disease, a newly discovered and little understood infection, possibly caused by a nematode that can prevent the leaves from processing chlorophyll. It's the middle of June and a grove of beech saplings near the dam look withered, their leaves browning and desiccated. Weakened, the trees become less resistant to pests and other stresses. "What's different here?" Lopane asks. Then, answering her own question: "It looks like winter." There is a fair amount of nonnative knotweed as well that isn't helping any.

Her mood lifts at the sight of some wild sarsaparilla, its leaves shaped like little umbrellas, which I can suddenly see everywhere. It is a native woodland wildflower, sows quickly, and is a fall plant. Can we get some seeds? Lopane asks Feinberg. And what about the white chervil? It's in the carrot family, good for pollinators, and likes shady floodplains. That could work here. And get musclewood on the list, it's a good floodplain tree. How about some jumpseed, a ground cover that can stabilize soil in moist areas? Feinberg nods. She likes the sound of jumpseed, a native knotweed that flowers in August and comes in on its own. Deer don't eat it, and it grows well on edge of trails. There are not many oaks here. Would they do well? Red oaks are added to the list of saplings to plant.

Feinberg is checking out the garlic mustard. It's not worth the effort to remove it if it's everywhere, which, she notes, it usually is. It's usually gone by July, but it still messes with the soil chemistry. "You pick your battles," she says with a sigh. Her reactions are decisive. The thickets of invasive honeysuckle draw her disdain, as does the barberry which she "would burn if I could." Ditto the ferns, which annoy her because they "need light, moisture, too much work." But she loves the tulip trees on the site, tall, massive, straight, some looking to be 100 or 200 years old. "They are just really happy here," she says. In her thirties, Lindsey went to Bard College, where she was an art student. "I didn't take any ecology courses," she tells me. With tall brown rubber boots, a fleece jacket, easy manner, and hair escaping its knot pulled back in a green tie, she exudes the genuine curiosity and resolve that often come with being self-taught. Studying art has helped her in recognizing plants. It's how she learned "to really look at things, how to pay attention," she tells me. It taught her patience as well.

Her words recall those of the poet Mary Oliver, who wrote in her essay "Upstream" that "Attention is the beginning of devotion." But they also evoke those of Sallie McFague, a feminist theologian who thought of divine presence in terms of the natural world. McFague wrote extensively about human stewardship and how questions of ecology and divinity might be more closely associated than we usually think, particularly in the way we see the world *as it is*: "The message is that we pay attention to difference, that we really learn to see what is different from ourselves. That is not easy. We can acknowledge a thing in its difference if it is important to us or useful to us, but realizing that something other than oneself is real, in itself, for itself, is difficult. To acknowledge another being as different—perhaps even indifferent to me, as for instance a hovering kestrel—is for most of us, a feat of the imagination." McFague drew a connection between deep attention and prayer, reflecting on the words of philosopher Simone Weill that "absolute attention is prayer."[7]

Lopane and Feinberg would likely be baffled if I suggested that they are praying, but their attention is absolute. Certainly they are perfectly attuned to difference, along with the indifference of the natural world. Without a doubt, too, their work is a feat of the imagination. And at the moment, it is just grass they are talking about! There are so many native grasses that could be used here, ones that like to stay short, that don't need mowing, Lopane muses. Delicate tufts of Pennsylvania sedge could work well, and Lindsey has already started to collect its seeds. What about broadleaf box grass?—it could be a good backbone plant. And maybe clumps of *Carex laxiflora*, a coarse perennial sedge, almost blueish in color. Near the dam itself, close to what could be a spoils area, tufts of *Carex swanii*, or swan's sedge, are already thriving. With narrow, flat leaves, the perennial grass does well in moist soil. Lindsey will collect more of its seeds. Native spicebush, or *Lindera*, is flourishing near the proposed third spoils area that is the largest. It may be a natural gulley. Maybe the spicebush seeds could be collected? It is added to the list. But all the trees are going to have to go. As will the garlic mustard, poison ivy, Christmas ferns, wineberry. "It's okay to just get rid of them," Lindsey says, concluding the recitation of the desired and the despised. It's not a prayer, exactly, but some sense of devotion is in play here, and their discourse lies somewhere between an appeal, a supplication, a meditation, and a hope.

Later that summer, I run into Suzette at our local Stop & Shop. She is doing her family shopping for the week, but tells me she is also bringing vegetables from her own garden to some of the employees at the store. The sense of exchange is typical with her. I tell her I find it hard to believe she has the time to garden, and she says, after a silence, "I can't imagine not having the time." She mentions as well that the permitting for removal has been delayed. She had submitted the application to NYSDEC back in January and is reluctant to send the job out for bids until the permits are fully in place. It's possible that notching the dam can start in the spring now. Though not especially pleased, she still seems unfazed. It may be a stretch, but I like to think that working with waterways gives her some intuitive understanding of the time it takes to get things done.

Permitting may be delayed, but that doesn't do much to slow research upstream of the site. On a beautiful clear morning in early September, I drive down to the site to check out what's going on with the fish count above the dam. The first person I see in the parking lot is Caleigh Millette, my friend from Shapp Pond. She's jazzed to be here and tells me she participated in the electrofishing a couple of weeks earlier below the dam. She's already putting on her waders and shares her excitement: On that previous outing, the team counted 150 or so eels, sunfish, suckers, and mitten crabs, too—nonnative, but not too invasive. The group of volunteers that gathers now includes a high school teacher, a couple of NYSDEC ecologists, a curator of wildlife management, and a handful of students, all of us there to meet up with Sarah Mount, an educator with NYSDEC. She'll be in charge of the electrofishing, a method of sampling and measuring fish populations that uses an electrical field to temporarily stun fish without harming them. From the outset, it is clear that Mount has a particular affection for eels and the fortitude and persistence they exhibit in their upstream passage. The numbers recorded today will add to data collected across fifteen years at this site.

Hatched in the saltwater currents of the Sargasso Sea, young eels migrate to the freshwater rivers and tributaries of the Northeast. Years later, they make the return passage to the ocean where they spawn and spend the remainder of their lives, a transoceanic journey that biologists have yet to fully understand. The health of the species depends on its ability to thrive in those freshwater tributaries—which means they need to be able to get upstream. And as Mount explains, "You lose eel density with every barrier." Over 150 eels had been counted below the dam. Today, we expect to see about twenty.

But if there are fewer eels above the dam, they will be bigger. Eels can and do make it around things, and as long as their skin is wet, it's possible for them to crawl around on land on a rainy night. Her hair pulled back in a casual ponytail, wearing a gray t-shirt and tan waders, Mount exudes practicality and is warm, capable, and informative with the manner of a practiced educator. She issues directions in a friendly, jargon-free, authoritative tone. She studied eels in college and started working for NYSDEC in 2010. It's clear that her admiration for the ingenuity of this fish that can find its way up and around a twenty-five-foot dam is one big reason she's here. Her enthusiasm is infectious.

Mount explains the protocols of electrofishing: The operator wears a backpack holding batteries and wields a long pole with the anode at the end, a cable holding the cathode trailing behind. That sends a small field of electricity into the water, stunning the fish just long enough for them to be netted and collected. Three netters work alongside the operator, collecting the fish, while two volunteers with buckets to hold the fish follow behind. While it's possible for participants to get a quick shock if their skin touches water, they're wearing rubber waders and long rubber gloves to prevent that. It's an active, fast-paced exercise, and the cardinal rule is communication: If you *do* slip into the water, do it loudly. Let the person wearing the backpack know so they can switch off the current. The backpack beeps and flashes a red light when the current is turned on.

It all requires attention, quick responses, and a degree of physical grace. Scoop the eels from downstream to upstream in an upward motion, Mount instructs. They'll try to jump out. Work together! Pinch the net closed to keep the eels in so you don't lose them in the transfer to the bucket. Make an eddy with the net if the eel is hidden behind a rock. Don't stick your hands in the water! Once they're in the bucket, put the lid on. The team will do three passes on this section of stream, expecting to collect the most fish on the first round, then fewer, then even fewer. We'll catch whatever we can, Mount says: eels, other fish, crayfish, crabs, turtles, all to get a sense of what's going on in the creek. After they've been identified and the eels counted, they will all be released. After a pause, she explains that the refraction of light on water can cause optical illusions, the fish being slightly closer and deeper than they appear to be. Along with the slick rocks on the bed of the creek and the slippery skin and scales of the samples to be collected, the whole enterprise is beginning to seem precarious.

The count takes place well above the impoundment in a narrow section of stream only fifteen or twenty feet wide, ten or twelve inches deep. A block net spanning the full width of the stream is installed at the bottom of the stream section. The length of the stream where the count is made is maybe a couple of hundred yards. It's a heavily invaded area: Jewelweed, purple loosestrife, mugwort, bamboo, and porcelain berry proliferate on the banks. Cabbage moths and butterflies flit around, and I see a brown butterfly with white spots on its wings. Mount and her volunteers start to work their way upstream, and shouts erupt in about thirty seconds when an eel is spotted. It slips away. But they get another one a minute or so later, put it in the net, pinch it shut, get it to the bucket, get the lid on. Mount yells "Shocker on!" whenever the current is switched on, and slowly they move up the stream, going back and forth across its width.

Some volunteers are practiced, others are novices. The flashing lights and continuous beeping of the backpack are in keeping with the sense of urgency here, the quick movement of catching fish this way. Fieldwork is so often a matter of patience, of silence, of waiting and quiet observation, but a whole different sensibility is in play here. Finding and netting the fish requires fast responses, swift and able partnerships, and the sense of excitement among the students is especially palpable. "Eel, eel, eel," I hear. "Deeper, Deeper, deeper." "Get it in the bucket, get it in the bucket, get it in the bucket." It's the repetition that comes naturally from excitement. "There are two of them, there are two of them, there are two of them!" They reach a rock wall below a house, where they know the eels like to take shelter and find habitat. An eel quickly goes into the bucket. All of it, along with the formation in which they are moving upstream on this bright morning, suggests a festive parade in tribute to stream diversity.

Meanwhile, a team on shore is continuing the species census, counting and identifying the eels, red breast and green sunfish, crayfish, the occasional snail, suckers, tiny catfish, fallfish, a large bass. Caleigh uses a small net to transfer the fish from the buckets to a larger plastic tub. An aerator puts oxygen in the water. It gurgles. Dan Aitchison, a curator of wildlife management, notes the advanced engineering of fieldwork instruments as he breathes into it.

Lindy is in the seventh grade, and currently she worries that the large bass in the tub will eat the smaller fish. The consensus among those present, however, is that the bass is probably too stressed out right now to have a snack. Lindy's red hair is woven into a braid worthy of a Renaissance painting, and if she was shy when the morning started, she is exhilarated to be part of the species identification program. Mount has traded in her role as the electrofishing director with another educator and is now sitting on an overturned orange compound bucket from Home Depot. With her elbows resting on her knees, she uses the opportunity of fish identification to conduct an impromptu seminar on aquatic species. What's this, she asks, picking out a small flat fish with rosy scales from the bucket. A redbreast sunfish, calls out Lindy. Next comes black nose dace. Lindy knows her invasive species and laughs while watching them jump around in the tub. Mount picks out a cutlip minnow and points out the distinct feature at its mouth. Then she tosses it into the tub. As she transfers a sucker into the tub, she says, "You have to hang on to these really tightly." She is at ease with holding and identifying these slithery, wiggling creatures, and the comedy of it enhances her outdoor classroom style. "Do eels have teeth?" Lindy asks suddenly. "They're stubby, like sandpaper, but they do," says Mount, as she holds up another small fish. "Golden shiner," says Lindy.

The captured, now writhing eels have been put in a separate water bucket infused with a few drops of clove oil, a natural local anesthetic that sedates them in a matter of minutes. The sluggish fish laze in the bottom of the bucket like teenagers getting stoned in a dorm room, activity and energy all but coming to a full stop. When they're doped up enough to be easily handled, volunteers take them out of the bucket one at a time to put on the fish board, counting and measuring them as they go. When Lindy takes a particularly large one out and stretches it out on the fish board, she murmurs, "They're softer than silk. How do they get so soft?" Her tenderness reminds me of what Fran Dunwell had said about kids and their innate affection for this species.

By the end of the afternoon, after three stream passes, the eel count comes to thirty-one, well above the twenty Mount had hoped for. Taking measure of events in the natural world often seems elusive, and at no time more so than when streaming water and slithering eels are involved. The number of fish, the distance they've travelled, the miles of restored stream, and all other such mathematical calculations can seem difficult to grasp, but in this age of data, a few numbers are certain. Since 2015, the estuary program has funded or participated in dam removal projects that have opened up twenty-six miles of upstream habitat. Although Mount tells me that one analysis has determined that there are 11,009 stream miles in the estuary, it's a start. And even she knows that "the data can be slippery, just like those eels."

Once measured and counted, the eels are put into the larger tub with the other fish before they're all returned to the stream. Not unexpectedly, fish diversity is higher above the dam. Eels can dominate—not in terms of predation but by taking up habitat and food resources—and with fewer eels upstream above the dam, the other fish are doing better. But none of these—not the eels, nor the sunfish, not the suckers, nor the bass—qualify as charismatic megafauna, the term of art for those species to which humans respond innately, directly, and emotionally. Conservationists and scientists depend on such species—pandas and polar bears, dolphins and cheetahs—and their possible extinction to engage public interest, imagination, and with any luck, a broader sense of stewardship. Now, looking at the kids counting and handling the various fish, I find myself suddenly and astonishingly hopeful about the fact that sometimes we humans come to value things simply through the act of looking for them. "Look how beautiful!" one of the kids says.

Only a few days later, I receive an email from Suzette. Things are moving along with the permits, she tells me, but they've hit a sandbar, or, more precisely, the level of pesticide chemical residues in the sediment behind the dam. Lopane is hoping to resubmit the data later in the fall but suggests a greater problem: "When we do the same testing on upland areas, we almost always find some levels of lead from the days of leaded gas. It was common practice that 'dilution is the solution' and so we accepted small levels of chemicals everywhere believing that in small doses they do no harm. We think differently today."

Concern about toxins in the sediment continues to hold up permit approval for months. Four tests above the dam had revealed traces of polycyclic aromatic hydrocarbons (PAHs), cancer-causing chemicals found in coal, crude oil, and gasoline coal; heavy metals such as lead, zinc, and copper; and residues from pesticides, including DDT and Chlordane. The silt in the impoundment behind the dam is very fine, and contaminants stick to the tiny particles. I am reminded that in the early twenty-first century there are no untouched sediments in this watershed. Jackman has noted that "Contaminants exist and persist behind dams; there are no pristine impoundments in our study and historical industrial activity is written into the sediment load."[8] With over 200 years of industry in the Hudson Valley, all these contaminants were widely used at one time or another. Additional samples will determine their presence downstream in the tidal area, further evidence of their widespread use in decades past.

It is the purpose of rivers to transport sediment. That's what they do. Let it flow out into the river. The flow carries nutrients into the ocean. "The sediments are a sort of epic poem of the earth," Rachel Carson wrote in her book *The Sea Around Us*. But she was talking about the ocean, outpourings from volcanoes, the embedded records of ice sheets, debris from flooding. What's happening here is not exactly an epic poem. "Say there are 30,000 cubic yards of it," Lopane says. "We can put 10,000 yards in the pits. But what do we do with the rest? It goes downstream? We dump it in Pennsylvania? In someone else's watershed? No. We put it where it is, we used it and made that choice." She'd like to see the scientific community face up to fact that "the world we live in is dirty. We are exploiters." Still, she knows that the community isn't oblivious, but uncertain and unresolved. Toxic sediments are known to be in the system, but their management remains site specific, depending on amounts and concentrations. And to date there is no clear formula or established standard for their disposal. Lopane's voice trails off, her frustration justified. She's asking what might be the chief existential question of our times. What do we do with the world we have created?

In early January 2024, I run into her in town. A forecast for the first major snow of the year later that day, six or eight inches, has brought in the crowds, but as we stand chatting, she tells me she is putting together her seed list for the spring. Such is her attention to time and seasons, and her natural inclination to look ahead. She tells me there are still no results from the downstream soil tests. They have to be equal to or worse than the ones above the dam. "Otherwise, I just don't know what we'll do," she says. "There has to be a better way. We've been at this for five years." But we both know that such regulatory oversight is vital to waterway management, and I remind her of the trout fisherman I've come across who mutter about blowing up the dams. "Well, nature is going to blow them up too," she says in exasperation. "There are thousands of these decrepit dams in the state. They're a safety hazard. A lot of them are a threat to downstream residents."

Besides, she reminds me, once the permits come in, it'll take another few months at least to get a range of bids from contractors. Habitat protection is another worry, and it places restrictions on in-water work. Because Indiana bats have established colonies in the woodlands and bald eagles nest in the upper reaches, those woods shouldn't be disturbed from mid-February to mid-September. Beyond that, it's not clear what the restrictions will be or how they will affect the timetable, and it's really only practical to take down trees in winter anyway. NYSDEC advocates for dam removal, yet such prohibitive measures make it difficult to map a clear path forward. To date, Riverkeeper has put in about $100,000 toward this project, with Westchester County spending about $250,000. "There has to be a better way," Lopane repeats.

Spring and summer of 2024 pass without permit approval. I know that the application has been submitted to multiple departments at the agency: The Bureau of Ecosystem Health biologists review for impacts to streams and wetlands; the Division of Water engineers look at potential impacts to water quality; and the Division of Materials Management will review it as well if the proposal involves removal of sediment for upland placement. The results of the sediment sampling will determine whether it is removed offsite to an approved disposal facility, stored on site, or allowed to wash downstream. No timetable is offered for completing the review, though a NYSDEC representative suggests in an email that it will be "soon," followed by the qualifier, "I'm not sure how soon is soon."[9] Her final words remind me of my first conversation with Scott Cuppett. "Whatever forever means," he had said then, and I am reminded again of the uncertainty that come with those things that happen in real time.

Lopane tells me that she looks increasingly to the "Resist, Accept, Direct" framework (RAD) used by the National Parks Service to determine how to address ecological challenges of a fast-changing world, whether those changes have to do with invasive species, residual toxins, or land use changes. It is a way of determining how much human intervention makes sense—at a time when any and all degrees of such intervention seem to be experimental. If resisting is a matter of adhering to historical conditions, accepting allows the ecosystem to evolve without intervention; directing works to actively influence change. Without offering specific instruction, it instead suggests a process by which to think through the questions. It occurs to me that in its straightforward simplicity, the framework echoes the prayer used in recovery programs—the serenity to accept, the courage to change, the wisdom to know the difference—although the supplication here is not on behalf of the individual but of a broader constituency. At Jamawissa, Lopane alternates between accepting and directing.

And so the weeks pass. As frustrating as the delays are, they reflect the reality in this kind of work; if cycles of rain and drought, of weather at large have become harder to predict, human interventions are just as difficult to anticipate. People go on breaks, they change jobs, and nothing in regulatory agencies has ever happened swiftly. While it is easy to understand changes in staffing and personnel, the holdups that come routinely within the bureaucracy of multiple regulatory agencies, and the complexity that comes with scientific review, the delay in permitting still seems excessive. It is hard not to make an association between this colossal dam with its massive buildup of sludge, sediment, and all its material inertia and the steady accumulation of weeks, months, and years now that it's taking for permit approval. The dam itself has become a symbol of stoppage, of stasis, of the immovable obstacle, the permanent impediment.

But when a dam breaches, it happens in real time, in the moment, without a time lag or digital delay. In late August, I come across two articles in *The New York Times* on the same day, an alignment of news stories that suggests—to me, anyway—certain inevitabilities. One is about a dam collapse in eastern Sudan; after severe rains, the Arba'at dam near the Red Sea failed, and flooding waters from its emptying reservoirs resulted in the deaths of at least 148 people and the damaging or destruction of the homes of roughly 50,000 people in twenty villages downstream. Two pages later, a different story documents the removal of four colossal hydroelectric dams on the Klamath River in southern Oregon and northwest California. Following years of litigation, a 249-mile stretch of that river will now flow freely, sediments flushed downstream and spawning grounds reopened with salmon soon to resume their swift migration.[10] Less than a month after removal was complete, hundreds of salmon were spotted swimming upstream to spawn in the cool creeks. The proximity of these two stories in the printed paper reflects their parallel realities, and I'm reminded of another truism I've encountered more than once on some of these sites: There is no permit review when a dam is brought down by natural forces.

Geoff Goll is more sanguine about the prolonged timetable and has reserved judgment on the permitting delays. As he tells me over the phone,

> The reality is that New York, especially the Hudson River valley, has gone through some pretty dramatic environmental disasters, especially in the river and the sediment with GE. So it makes sense that they're extremely sensitive to the health of the river. These people are dedicated to protecting the environment. But you can't be a master of everything, right? They're trying to do what they can with the regulations. And I can tell you, they want to figure out how to approve this. They're just trying to figure out a way to work within their regulations to make it happen. Like I said before it's the staffing turnover, things like that, I think it's out of their control. And so they want to do the right thing. They want to make sure that what they approve is going to protect the resources that they're required to protect."

Of the most recent exchange, he says "It was like they were trying to understand what the quality of that material was and we were trying to understand what they needed to get to allow them to progress. I think it's going to take some time."

As Jackman has said, "Every dam that comes down threatens the one upstream." He's seen the eels and herring downstream and knows that with the large Jamawissa dam removed, they'll get just a bit further up the tributary. "We want this to be a contagious movement," he has said. Still, I know that the next barrier, the dam that makes Railroad Pond created over a century ago to service the rail station—is barely a mile upstream. Con Edison, a more recent landowner, had used the property for power lines. The utility company, however, had been cited by NYSDEC for safety violations and, after first agreeing to repair the dam, ultimately decided instead to drain the pond and restore the waterway back to its original brook.

Beauty Reconsidered | 131

The nature of the contaminants embedded in its sediment were unknown, however, and local residents preferred to preserve the view of the lake; they remembered skating there as kids, they'd had their wedding photos taken there. A community group created a Facebook page for its preservation and signed a petition citing, perhaps predictably, the ecology and biodiversity of the pond and its adjacent wetlands as an argument for preservation. To be fair, the ecological benefits of dam removal were not widely recognized then; NYSDEC only began to offer grants in 2016. In 2011, the town raised the $300,000 to buy the fifty-five acres of lake and watershed area from Con Edison, with the utility company paying for repairs. Today the area is maintained as a passive recreation area by the town. The day I visit, though, it's difficult to find the way to the pond. One small trail leads to a grassy clearing with a couple of overturned rowboats next to a stagnant pool of water with a skim of duckweed. An access road a few hundred yards downstream that leads to the dam is gated. I can walk past it, but none of it seems to read much as a community amenity, and certainly no one is using it on this bright September afternoon.

November 2024 passes without permit approval. Instead, NYSDEC has asked for additional samples. The quality of toxins in the downstream sediment had come in at roughly the same classification as those sediments above the dam. But had the sampling gone deep enough? And what would be the effect of sediment release on downstream biota? "What's the point of doing more sampling? How many more tests do you need?" Lopane asks in frustration. She considers whether the removal might simply be done in phases. The original plan had been to put a third of the sediment in spoils areas on the site, with the remaining two-thirds swept into the stream. Now she considers a partial dam removal that would allow two-thirds of the sediment to remain in the impoundment, with the final third to be removed and put in dredge areas on the site.

The strategy doesn't leave any provision for fish passage, but Lopane is determined to salvage the project. She's trying to be proactive and is looking for research to satisfy NYSDEC, reaching out to like-minded colleagues who are exploring aquatic biodiversity, conservation planning, and the socioeconomics of dam removal. Anyone there have a useful data base? She attends seminars on sediment management and filing grant applications. At the same time, though, her budget for the project is running low. "Now I have to dig fifteen feet below the surface of the sediment? And pay for a machine that can do that? I don't do long-form research on sediment! That's why I am doing all this reaching out. And yeah, of course they are scared." And she returns to the idea of trying to get a permit for phasing the project.

Geoff Goll had told me about the vision he had for the site.

> You look at the surrounding landscape and what that looks like and the current water body that's there. One of the reasons they likely put that dam there is there is a nice constriction in the valley walls, bedrock there and very steep. So I would envision it's going to be sort of like a ravine. Then I always try to look twenty, thirty years later, and the forest will come down to where the steam is right now or where it will be once the dam is removed. So I think it will be really pretty, sort of like a little hidden ravine in that area once the dam is out.

But I recall just as clearly his forecast: "You're doing what you can based simply on all your experience and education and expertise to take that data and then say OK, we believe this is how the river is going to react when we remove the dam. And so that is sort of like a prediction."

Whether you call it a vision or a prediction, the view to the future here remains unsure. But I wonder if the wearisome delays and protracted schedule also reflect our own uncertainties about what we hope to find in the natural landscape as our expectations and standards shift. The dam dismantled signals evolving ideas of how we define beauty in landscape, and they go from artificial shaping of landscape to a less mannered relationship with earth and water. The dam and its pond were created to conform to Gilded Age aesthetics: formal manicured gardens with classical layouts, exotic flowers and shrubs, sculpted bushes and trees. They were designed for private viewing and the pleasure of the few.

That property now serves as a park and conservation area open to the public, its reflecting pond on its way to being a free-flowing stream, a nursery and habitat for fish and wildlife species repaired. Our emerging aesthetic today has more to do with restoring a kind of order to things, a relationship with natural systems that is not about reforming and reconfiguring them, but rather finding a coherence, possibly even a sense of accord, existing between the human and natural worlds. If such an effort comes with difficult terms, unknown conditions, and indefinite timetables, it is also one that suggests our human ideas of order can coalesce with those of natural systems—a confluence of discrete sensibilities not unlike the way the flowing creek merges with the river current just downstream.

Figure 6. The excavator breaks through the Sprout Creek dam and the fish win.

Streams Reconnected

> If I were called in
> To construct a religion
> I should make use of water
>
> —Philip Larkin[1]

Just north of where I live, the Hudson River School of painting was established in the mid-nineteenth century by Thomas Cole, Frederick Edwin Church, Sanford Gifford, and others. Their subjects were not just mountains, crags, luminous skyscapes, and waterfalls but our place in them. These artists painted the banks of the river and the rise of the Catskills, the skies above them, views of the New World that ranged from pastoral pleasures to transcendent visions. As a place of allegory, the landscape offered inspiration and revelation, and the paintings worked to capture that imagined association between the extravagant beauty of the natural world and the emerging nation. That the American character was shaped by sublime wilderness and all its radiant infinities was suggested with such assurance that one could almost believe it. Tiny figures in a monumental landscape imply that human presence is small in the grand sweep of nature, though an occasional puff of smoke might hint at the enterprise and intrusion of the railway. Some historians speculate that the extravagant crimson and violet sunsets documented the chemicals being burned in the furnaces of the various industrial concerns established along the river, but that was of no matter then. From the serene to the sublime, these paintings were studies of how the human figure might be accommodated by the great sweep of seemingly uncultivated nature, useful exercises in the new country's efforts to establish its cultural identity.

Almost two centuries later, the most accurate visual renderings of how we see ourselves in the landscape are found elsewhere. Possibly it is in the selfies in which visitors to majestic natural formations take their own photos, assigning themselves a central place in the view to the mountain ledge or cataract, thus reducing the natural world to a picturesque background, scenery for the self. But an even more apt representation might be found in all those Zoom meetings so many of us have attended in recent years. Where I live, participants who choose not to be seen in their own homes or offices frequently opt instead for a virtual background, selecting some familiar landscape—the wide, slate-gray Hudson River or the forested hills that bracket its banks. I've done it myself. When viewing a fellow Zoom attendee against such a backdrop, the sense of displacement can be jarring. The shape of the participant's head, the profile, the outline, even strands of hair are incomplete, cut off, vague, warped, emphasizing the disconnection with the virtual landscape. What we see most of all is an image of dislocation, people pretending to be situated in a place they are not.

That sense of displacement surfaced elsewhere as well, as on the summer afternoon I took a river ride with some friends on the upper Hudson. We were on a small commercial cruise boat that offered tours of the riverscape and shoreline, and it included a running narrative of the landmarks seen on both. But the voice-over was recorded and frequently out of sync with what we were seeing along the waterway and shoreline—a lavish description, say, of the historic home of a celebrated Dutch landowner when we were actually passing a landfill, or a shipyard described as a factory. It might have only been off by a minute or two, but the sense of disconnect was both weird and profound. And very real, too, in how it captured the way we can think we are in one place when we are in another. And how our assumptions of place don't always align with where we actually are.

A face that is out of place, a voice that is out of sync. Both seem representative of our current relations with the natural world, ones marked by a sense of dissonance and disconnection.

A like sense of disruption is a constant in so many of the cycles known to us—of seasons, of temperature, of rain and snow, in the unsettling sound of spring birdsong in January, in the sight of a black bear lumbering across the road in a warm December, in the melodic mating call of peepers in the wetlands arriving in early March, or in the maple trees that my friend in Vermont tapped two weeks earlier this February than she had a year ago. Scientists are also speculating that nonnative animal species are better able to adapt to changing environmental conditions—extreme heat, drought, intense storms—than native species, which tend to be less physiologically adaptable and more susceptible to disturbances. As unexpected species appear in unexpected places, they reconfigure familiar ecosystems—another sign of displacement, another blow to biodiversity. When established patterns of habitat, food, and species migration are interrupted, they cause ecological mismatches that throw us out of whack.[2]

As functioning human beings, we all generally learn to cope with unpredictable events, experiences, behaviors. But when such disruptions occur on a global scale, one that is social, atmospheric, environmental, biological, it is destabilizing in a larger and more existential way. Names for the psychological range of effects go from the generic to the clinical. The emerging field of climate psychology studies the effects of environmental change on the human psyche and calls this condition *systemic uncertainty*. Biologist E. O. Wilson coined the term *biophilia* in the mid-1980s, but before his death in 2021, he also was also known to use the term *eremocene*, meaning the age of loneliness characterized by a disengagement from natural species and natural cycles.

A 2023 study in the Yale Journal of Biology and Medicine observed that "Insecurity, danger, chaos, and an unstable system due to climate change have both short- and long-term psychological effects." *Solastalgia* describes the existential distress—newly identified conditions such as eco-anxiety, ecological grief, climate work, and climate trauma—and that sense of overall disconnection we confront in a transformed natural world.[3] Factor in the field day that social scientists have in conjecturing on the causes and character of broader social discordance: In a population isolated and atomized by the dispiriting effects of social media, political divisions, flourishing consumerism, and technological dehumanization, it's no surprise that people spend more time alone.

In the emerging field of environmental neuroscience, researchers are learning how extreme temperatures have neurological as well as psychological effects that vary from irritability to cognitive dysfunction. Extreme heat fosters not only ennui and fatigue but aggression and violence as well. Algae blooms and toxins in water can lead to neurogenerative diseases. Post-traumatic stress disorder (PTSD) is a result not only of wartime trauma but of exposure to climate crises—wildfires, flooding, tornados, hurricanes, and the catastrophic after-effects of superstorms. Epidemiologists are beginning to learn that disorders in ecosystems can lead to the shifting populations of insects, birds, and bats, all climate refugees themselves with an aptitude for spreading disease. Our neural pathways can be disrupted and otherwise altered by a warming climate in ways only beginning to be understood today.[4]

I suspect my abiding interest in reconnecting tributaries has to do with this sense of disconnection. Reconsidering the value of continuity seems timely. With the natural world and with one another, of course. Connectivity gives shape and meaning to our lives. It is not just a matter of connecting separate segments of a single whole, as can happen in streams and rivers, but also in other more disparate areas—ideas, things, people, practices, species, sometimes even self and others—that don't seem to belong together. Until they do. We know that social connection is vital to human health. That connection can be an interior process too, the intersection of thought and feeling, or a decision reverberating with unexpected consequences, or in the way past experience anticipates current behavior. It's how we make sense of things. Reflecting on the work of Barry Lopez, Rebecca Solnit writes: "If disconnection is the devastation that allows an abuser to abuse, a family to deny, a child to suffer in silence, connection is itself curative."[5]

Certainly that sense of curative connection was something I encountered across the sites I visited and the people working around them. It was in the associative thinking that moves David Rothenberg to create improvisational concerts that fuse recordings of aquatic insects and plants with the notes of his clarinet. It's the kind of inclusive thinking that motivates Fran Dunwell to set up an education program for kids to help search out the ways in which the health of the estuary is affected by eel passage in the tributaries. It is in the way Geoffrey Goll does his best to determine the flow of a channel by looking to both the past and future of the site.

And it is the kind of integrated thinking that prompts Laura Wildman to reach out to bioengineers found on the American Fisheries Society listservs to learn how to integrate the needs of another species into her engineering practice. Or simply channeling Frank Lloyd Wright and asking, "How is the site is speaking to me?" "I'm really a networking engineer," she told me. "There is no solution I can come up with completely on my own. I just feel the answer is going to be better, more complete, more accurate if I ask other people."

The connections can be unexpected and incidental. In my own life, a project documenting our town's natural resources, a dam breach just down the road, and the pandemic lockdown formed a constellation of circumstances that led me to these waterways and their impoundments.

All of these, it seems to me, qualify as intuitive human responses to systemic uncertainty. I would like to think that connectivity, whether momentary or lifelong, is a fundamental human impulse and one we search it out instinctively. We may even be hardwired for it, for that innate appreciation of one thing leading to another and that to another. Maybe the fact that the human body is 75 percent water accounts for that intrinsic bond we have with the water world. Maybe it's just our own circulatory systems that allow us to have some innate grasp of flow and of unhindered currents. Laura Wildman takes the analogy further, saying "It's just like all those dynamic amazing things going on in our bodies with cells and growth and blood and transport. The earth is the exact same way. It is a large living organism that is all connected."

"As human beings, we are part of the whole stream of life," Rachel Carson said in 1954 to a gathering of women journalists.

Certainly that connectivity is becoming evident elsewhere across the American landscape, as in the emerging science of road ecology and the growing prevalence of culverts, underpasses, and overpasses planted with shrubs and trees. Such crossings folded into human infrastructure allow other species to find their way over or under roadways that otherwise bisect habitat and migration, and they include tunnels for toads, bridges for pronghorn antelopes, highway underpasses for ocelots, and "fences" constructed of native trees and plants that offer food, shelter, and nectar for birds, insects, and butterflies passing through. It is an emerging ethos that recognizes how fragmented landscapes and waterways disturb both animal populations and the natural cycles of food, migration, and reproduction that they depend upon. The Bipartisan Infrastructure Law passed in 2021 acknowledged the need for human transportation corridors to provide for wildlife habitat and secure passage, and funding has since become available to state, local, tribal, and regional agencies to provide for the right-of-way of other species.[6]

Whether it is a thruway overpass or a concrete dam, perhaps the reassessment of barriers in the built world is a way of practicing something that comes naturally to us. Perhaps it can serve as a template for restoring continuity. Following our inborn impulses all too often leads to damage and spoils, whether it is in squandering resources, degrading habitats, or spewing pollutants across air, land, and water. Yet if it is innately human to search out connectivity, perhaps this is a time when we can look to our own tendencies to do the right thing instead of the wrong thing. Perhaps our native appreciation for connectivity can also motivate us to serve the health of our waterways. Perhaps self-interest and broader social interest are not mutually exclusive. Perhaps this is one of those rare instances in which there is a simultaneity of purpose, in which human interests can be congruent with, rather than disruptive to, the ecological interests of the natural world.

All dams are temporary, George Jackman has said. One dam, one stream, one mile, one year at a time.

I find that the mechanics of continuity are ever more present in my mind. It can begin anywhere, as with the removal of a dam midway along the tributary.

And it can be ephemeral, as in those temporary headwaters that flow only for a short time, yet affect the character of everything downstream.

Flow and discontinuity are not mutually exclusive. Flow need not be uniform and consistent. A free-flowing stream can be erratic, inconsistent, nonlinear, multidirectional, lateral as well as longitudinal, unseen. Just as connectivity can be illogical, out of sequence, unexpected.

Ecologist and theologian Sallie McFague writes about such connections. *Eremocene* and *species loneliness* were not terms used at the time of her writing in the 1990s, but her thinking anticipates them when she writes about the schism between the internal human world we treat as subject and the external material world we view as object. And it is a deepening divide that characterizes our current disordered relations with the environment. McFague suggests that that the way in which we assign the term *natural resources* to the environment at large reveals an objectification of nature. She advocates instead for the realignment of spirit that occurs when one enters an I-Thou relationship, as imagined by Martin Buber, rather than an I-It relationship. Buber writes in his book *I and Thou*: "There is nothing that I must not see in order to see, and there is no knowledge that I must forget. Rather is everything, picture and movement, species and instance, law and number included and inseparably fused. Whatever belongs to the tree is included: its form and its mechanics, its color and its chemistry, its conversation with the elements and its conversation with the stars—all this in its entirety."[7]

Buber believed that people could enter into a relationship of mutuality in their encounters not only with other people but with things and nature and that when we recognize the other—whether it is another person, an inanimate object, a scrap of mica, or a tree—to be "you" rather than "it," a more profound affiliation can develop. For Buber, "you" signaled a broader and more humane appreciation of language and offered a form of address that could lead to an understanding, an intimacy, a deeper awareness of the mysteries and unpredictable wonder in the world outside of ourselves. As such, the use of the second person pronoun replaces discrete object with connected subject and values not abstract knowledge and information, but the reciprocal partnership and dialogue one can enter into with the natural world.

In 2024, I come across assorted blueprints for that partnership. Designer Russell Maxwell had moved from New York City with his wife and daughters to the small city of Beacon, New York, in 2020. He was trained as a cartographer at the University of Wisconsin in Madison but had spent much of his life designing graphics for financial institutions. Beacon is situated at the mouth of the Fishkill Creek, and Maxwell had found it a good place to take up the fishing he had done as a boy in North Carolina. Searching out public access sites along the creek, he was happy to catch "pretty much anything that bites."

Soon after, he started to map the creek. "I was just seeing it in little snippets and found I wanted to see it in its totality," he tells me when we meet in town on an April afternoon. Maxwell continued to fish, but he also walked the creek wherever he could, searching out parks and public access. Where there was no access, he often relied on his own drive-bys, turning as well to topographical maps, Google Maps, aerial photographs from local parcel access maps, and a variety of other documents from state and federal agencies.

Situating the dams on the creek was a challenge, and the maps provided by the state for environmental management agencies and rendered by engineers with technical backgrounds were of little help. "It was hard to extract the information," he says, and on the maps he later emails me dams are often indicated by dots that are so large it is difficult to know where they actually might be. Colors, icons, little flags, lines, dotted lines, and the general extravagance of imagery make for a graphic cacophony. "My main goal was to be able to *see* the creek from headwater to mouth without being distracted by roads and power lines, and names, and golf courses, and bike trails, and other streams, and towns, and major highways, and so forth. And then to establish a clear visual hierarchy without too much information, competing imagery and icons, all trying to show too many things."

Maxwell traced over the maps to create a single continuous rendering of the creek from its source at Pray Pond to where it flows into the Hudson River in Beacon. Waterways, roads, and railroads are all hand drawn, the weight of their lines wavering from time to time. Text includes a brief account of the creek's path, accompanied by images of its endangered species—Blanding's turtles, bog turtles, least bitterns, pie-billed grebes. He also included illustrations of the smallmouth bass, bluegill, yellow perch, and brown trout he has caught on the creek, not rendered by a program or an app but with the human hand. It may not be perfect, Maxwell admits, "but I wanted that warmth there. What I wanted was to be able to stand six feet away and see the whole creek all the way down, the entire length of the creek, from beginning to end."

Maxwell hung the map, measuring four by six feet, in his bedroom and would look at it first thing in the morning. Over time, he printed several different versions, finally settling on one that indicated the creek in a clear blue continuous stream of color varying in width. "Roads are predominant on most maps," he says. "Maps are made for roads, but I wanted roads to be secondary [to the creek]. It took hundreds of hours." Maxwell's map may be a labor of love, but as a hand-drawn visual artifact, it serves as a tangible alternative to digital navigation tools more common today and is now used by the Fishkill Creek Watershed Alliance as a document for water and floodplain management and as an educational tool for stakeholders and the public at large. "People still love maps," Maxwell tells me.

"I'm not a riparian expert," he continues, "but I've connected with the creek in an interesting and rewarding way. I have some savored moments fishing the creek, a beautiful bald eagle flying by upstream while fishing all alone—I heard its wings 'whapping' first and had no idea what it would be—a magical moment." Maxwell's phrasing starts to follow its own episodic current.

> A large, strange fish swimming upstream, maybe three feet long, just a shadow below the surface, could never figure out what it was, maybe a sturgeon, but above two dams from the Hudson? One day suddenly catching trout after trout—must have been ten or so in an hour period . . . then barely catching one again in several years of fishing the same spot . . . finding a strange volcanic rock on the shore down below the Texaco dam . . . finding all kinds of bones and skulls . . . startling deer on an island in Madam Brett park . . . wading along the creek, walking upstream and coming across a huge Great Blue Heron also wading and fishing!! I had to laugh . . . and on and on . . . I've spent many hours with a pole along the creek.

If Maxwell isn't quite in a conversation with the stars and with the elements, certainly his words reflect the flow of the stream and its species as subject rather than object.

Maxwell's map is one blueprint for continuity. Another, perhaps more prosaic, is the 2024 Dutchess County Natural Resources Inventory (NRI) that includes predictions about changing temperatures, changing precipitation, and the effects of sea level rise on the Hudson River and its tributaries, which is to say, the greater frequency and extent of coastal flooding that will put tidal communities along the river at risk. And while not advocating for dam removal explicitly, it mapped floodplain acreage, identified lakes and ponds exceeding twenty-five acres, and highlighted the ecological value of wetlands.

Another is the Action Agenda Plan for 2020 to 2025 developed by the Hudson River Estuary Program. It recognizes that rising temperatures, shifts in salinity and water depths, and the potential loss of tidal wetland and vegetation acreage caused by climate change affect aquatic movement and habitat. Acknowledging that the health of the tributaries is intrinsic to the health of the watershed at large, the plan itemized culverts and dams as impediments to fish and wildlife passage and the ways in which their deteriorating state causes flooding, interrupts flow, inhibits wildlife movement, and degrades habitat. The removal of barriers is a priority in its commitment to healthy tributaries.

"I think it's going to be a slow but steady process," Fran Dunwell had told me that day at her kitchen table. "As you have more and more success stories of dam removal and people can look at it and say 'Oh, this is beautiful too,' and they can see that the algae blooms are gone, that the wildlife is thriving, that they can have personal emotional experiences with a stream in the same way that they can with a lake. It'll take time." Sustained funding is critical, she adds.

> People decide to invest energy in something if they know there's a pretty good chance they can be rewarded for their efforts. If you have a grant program that you're continually changing, you know that's not a priority anymore. Developing the expertise and the projects for dam removal is a long-term process, and if the funding is fickle, it's hard to develop that expertise and the relationships and the project plans to move forward. If your partners—the individual landowners, the researchers, the outreach people—know this is a steady, sustained commitment that's going to be there, let's say for ten years, they're much more willing to put their own effort into it.

Those efforts are underway around the country. In June 2024, the Department of the Interior issued "Tribal Circumstances Analysis," a report acknowledging the comprehensive damage inflicted by hydroelectric dams built at the turn of the last century on the Columbia River and the Tribal Nations in that river basin. With their habitats fragmented or completely vanished, populations of wild salmon, steelhead, and native resident fish had all diminished, while land, ancestral burying rounds, and other sacred sites had all been lost to flooding. A partnership between the federal government and the affected nations was also formed to help restore an abundant population of salmon; to expand clean energy production; and to work toward some degree of stability for those communities in which agriculture, energy, transportation, and cultural traditions had been devastated by the fragmented river.

The ecological rewards of dam removal are increasingly recognized in watersheds elsewhere in New York State. In the north, near the Canadian border, the Saint Regis Mohawk Tribe spearheaded the effort to decommission and remove the 1929 Hogansburg Dam on the St. Regis River. The 2016 removal and restoration project reconnected 555 upstate river and stream miles of habitat for migratory species and was a land reclamation initiative that returned the immediate region from one of declining industries—hydropower, manufacturing, mining, timber mills—to a robust ecology more consistent with the history and practices of Mohawk tribal tradition.

Closer to home in the Hudson River watershed, the streams are conforming just a bit more to what I saw on those GIS maps in 2020. In Beacon, planning has started for the removal of the Tioronda dam. Five to seven feet high and 210 feet long, the stone and concrete first barrier dam tops a series of natural cascades, and its hydropower was put to use by the Tioronda Hat Works just downstream. The factory has long been abandoned, and beyond its crumbling brick buildings, the creek widens, then braids its way past tidal flats into the river. Today, the dam's owner is in conversation with Riverkeeper about removal and the effort is gathering support from regulatory agencies and the community. Sampling for aquatic life and sediment and water quality monitoring have begun, and plans for engineering designs will be the necessary next step.

Upstream is the Roundhouse Dam, the liability of which came into full focus in the summer of 2023 when a woman took a fatal fall down a fifteen-foot embankment into the rush of the Fishkill Creek while having her picture taken. The barrier and its picturesque falls are hard to resist for people unaware of the dangers that may come when centering themselves in front of impressive bits of landscape. Discussions for its removal have started. In early 2024, the National Fish and Wildlife Foundation awarded Riverkeeper a $3.87 million grant to remove the century-old first barrier

Holden Dam on the Quassaick Creek in Newburgh, New York, just across the river. Flash flooding from rain events, due to the high proportion of impervious surface in the nearby urban community, had caused bank erosion and the destabilization of the city's main sewer line. Its removal is expected to restore two miles of freshwater habitat, enhance flood resilience, and further fish passage.

~

On a chilly November morning in 2024, I head down to Sprout Brook in Cortlandt, New York. Permits from the Army Corps and NYSDEC have recently been signed, clearing the way for the removal of the Sprout Creek dam, a first barrier dam in Westchester County. The brook itself is not much more than twenty feet in width. It flows into Annsville Bay, a tidal area fed by a couple of other streams before emptying into the Hudson River. The dam was built in the 1950s to flood the area and create a private swimming club called Sprout Lake, a much-loved local asset with a sand beach, food concession, diving boards, and a big water slide. Decades later, as the area silted in and became a marshy wetland, Sprout Lake was abandoned. Ultimately, the town elected to fill it in for lacrosse and soccer fields, and piped water from the creek to irrigate the playing fields.

Only about five feet high and eighty feet long, the dam may be too low for a hazard rating, but it's not too small to block fish passage, and its removal will allow for a mile and a quarter of restored habitat, a five-fold increase over the present quarter mile of freshwater from dam to tide. The Hudson Valley Stream Conservancy (HVSC), a local nonprofit organization advocating for stream restoration, has spearheaded the removal, and Gareth Hougham, its president, has worked tirelessly to coordinate permits, water and soil sampling, funding, and the inevitable scheduling conflicts.

Hougham studied chemistry and environmental science in college, going on to be awarded a doctorate in polymer and physical organic chemistry. After spending thirty years in research at IBM, working with synthetic materials that weren't doing much for the environment, he founded HVSC in 2006. The conservancy's mission is to foster fish migration, work with towns to raise awareness of their small streams and reduce sewage pollution, and to increase public access to the Hudson River. Today, Hougham is also an adjunct professor of environmental science at SUNY Purchase, where he keeps a dedicated water quality lab and simply calls the five years he has given to this removal "a perseverance game." His credentials for this work actually go back further. A local, he remembers swimming in Sprout Lake as a kid. People were attached to the pond, he tells me, and he is aware as anyone that taking down the dam has been a contest of priorities. "Every dam removal is," he says.

On this November morning, a confederacy of stream advocates has convened, some because of their direct involvement in this project, others because, well, another dam is coming down, and that's not something to miss. Scott Cuppett is there, and so are John Waldman and George Jackman. Naturalist Stephen Stanne from Hudson River Sloop Clearwater is taking it all in, as is James Creighton, the deputy supervisor in Cortlandt. Suzette can't make it—she's planting grasses and shrubs in a saltwater marsh on the Long Island Sound that day. Laura Wildman isn't there either, but her fingerprints are on this job; she did the initial engineering plan, and her knowledge figured into consideration of how that soccer field was going to work out as a floodplain. The gathering of thirty-five or forty also represents a broader constituency of funders and supporters ranging from the Hudson River Estuary Program, Scenic Hudson, the Hudson River Foundation, Riverkeeper, Clearwater, to Matthew Castro, Principle Environmental Planner of Westchester County and the Westchester Soil and Water Conservation District, to people from local municipalities, board members, educators, volunteers, and a local television crew. A sense of shared purpose and enterprise make the anticipation palpable. Temporary orange mesh construction fencing, the bright yellow caution tape marking the site, and coffee and bagels from Dunkin add to the sense of festivity.

A temporary ramp made of rocks has been put down to allow passage for the hydraulic excavator, outfitted with a "breaker," that is going to drill into the concrete of the five-foot dam and smash it into bits. Josh Wilson is a senior ecologist from Biohabitats, the engineering firm managing this removal, and he tells me sampling hasn't turned up any evidence of contaminants, making this a "dream of a dam removal." "The stream will migrate," he says now, and a pool that has formed just below the dam is likely to vanish. After a heavy rainstorm a couple of years earlier, water had topped the dam, washing a significant amount of sediment downstream—that may create a few bars, but the channel is expected to generally maintain its route. The Biohabitats team has given the job a two-week window, but it's probably only going to take a couple of days to finish breaching the dam and another week or so to haul off the debris.

The drought in the Northeast in the fall of 2024 has made for dry conditions and low water, which helps. The excavator has made a couple of cuts in the center chunk of the dam, but the concrete is dense, and there's more rebar in it than anticipated. I know by now that these legacy dams can be mysterious, their interior construction materials anything from old farm tools to timber framing and, now, an excess of rebar. Dams can be a timeline of river history, but that's not a good enough reason to keep them in place.

Nothing dramatic happens. There is no sudden rush of silt or cascade of water. Some of the stream water has already been trickling under the dam. But then suddenly everything is moving in sync—the jerky ballet of the excavator arm, the tumble of smashed concrete, and the little cloud of concrete dust billowing up over it, the air and earth alike vibrating from the drilling. At 11:40 a.m., the water finds its way through. Such is the choreography of restoration. Sprout Brook is just then a little less fragmented. A few people on the bank clap. "That's what continuity is all about," says SUNY Purchase Environmental Studies Chair Professor Ryan Taylor.

It being November, the herring are out in the Atlantic Ocean, but Hougham knows there are eels in the stream just below the dam. In particular, one large, mature female yellow eel. Hougham has named her Georgie, in honor of George Jackman, and tells me Georgie is just "there waiting." Eels tend to stay put in a small area once they've settled in, and this one may not move upstream. But Hougham likes to imagine her welcoming in the tiny glass eels in the coming spring, directing them upstream to habitats not open to her when she first settled here years ago.

Five years and forty minutes; seemingly forever and then immediate; infinite delays and sudden momentum. These are yet more iterations of how things happen in real time, something that seems to keep finding new ways to reveal its changeability.

That same day, by coincidence, there happens to be an article in *The New York Times* about the unprecedented speed of change in the natural world and our inability to make sense of it. Twenty-first-century technology notwithstanding, data cannot be collected and analyzed at a rate that keeps up with climbing temperatures, sea level rise, and species extinction, as all of these are occurring more rapidly than anticipated. Climate research is especially behind, with warming temperatures breaking records almost monthly. "It turns out that we do not have systems in place to explore the significance of shorter-term phenomena in the climate in anything approaching real time," the authors write. "The data that went into the latest round of climate model simulations are based on observations that only run through 2014, and so they don't reflect recent changes such as newer pollution controls, volcanic eruptions or even the effects of Covid. Similarly, the forecasts are stuck with scenarios that were common in the early 2000s. Business (and everything else) has changed sharply since then." Advocating for more efficient modeling and faster data collection from satellites, they also suggest that if economic data takes years to analyze, estimates that are "good enough" and assumptions that are reasonable can be made.[8]

On this particular November morning, though, the stream threading its way in ordinary and familiar real time through the concrete chunks seems promising. It is nothing more than a trickle at first, but as the breaker continues to hammer at the concrete, splintering it into bits, the stream picks up speed and strength. Call it movement, momentum, brief evidence of our ability to restore some natural order of things.

Hyperconnectivity is another word recently added to the contemporary lexicon, and it refers to the tendency many of us have to be connected to multiple digital devices at a time, and to have information coming to us from a variety of different sources simultaneously: social media feeds, news outlets, in-person exchanges, data drops. I am tempted to dismiss the word as more needless new jargon. But watching the thin trickle of water widen and gain in volume and velocity as it streams through the smashed concrete, I imagine how that word could have broader relevance and meaning when applied to rivers and streams.

It is easy now to imagine a more appealing expression of hyperconnectivity. Wynants Kill, Jamawissa, Wappinger, Fishkill, Sprout Brook. After all this time, these names run together in my mind. Some of them are taken from the words used by Native Americans, others by later Dutch settlers. I know they are nothing but small tributaries in a single watershed with names that have little to do with each other. But their confluence in my mind takes me to the John Ashbery poem, "Into the Dusk-Charged Air," a recitation of the world's great rivers. The poem catalogs them in 151 lines, one after the other, all of them there: the Nile, the Niagara, the Hudson, Volga, Seine, Liffey, the Rhine and the Rhone and Rio Grande. The names and verbs may read like a list, yet on it goes with a relentless force, like the rivers themselves, the names falling over your tongue like water over rocks. With repetition and line breaks, Ashbery has captured inevitability, tenacity, natural force, expected and unexpected as in the flow of water itself.

It is a list of rivers in which one after the other is connected in the poet's imagination, each flowing into the next, strewn with rocks, blown by the wind, shallow and light-filled, or crusted with snow. The sound of their names connects them, too, along with the sound of their flow. When they are not frozen, stilled in winter, they are streaming, sidling, coursing into and alongside one another with a fluid momentum that allows the reader to believe in a kind of profuse continuity that is, if not geographically accurate, certainly present in the human psyche. And that continuity, I know by now, follows its own timeline and logic. Hyperconnectivity of a different order, it can start anywhere—at the source, near the headwaters, or anywhere in between.

In that way, the stories of these tributaries go on. None of these narratives have come to their conclusion. A year from now, five years from now, their stories will be different, continuing far beyond this final paragraph. Furnace Pond continues to stream through the fissures in the dam that tries to hold it back, but that may change. Two miles of the newly restored Jamawissa will flow uninterrupted into the Hudson River. The Fishkill Creek is impeded by one less dam than it was a decade ago. The tiny glass eels that make it to Sprout Brook each spring will find their way another mile or so upstream. What Buber calls the conversation with the elements goes on and on between these waterways and the communities they run through. Water continues to find its way.

Notes

From the Millpond to the Stream

1. Barry Lopez, "Lessons from the River," in *Embrace Fearlessly the Burning World: Essays* (Random House, 2022), 290.
2. Fred Alm, board president of the Burden Iron Works Museum, conversation with author, June 25, 2024.
3. John Lipscomb, *One Dam at a Time*, directed by Jon Bowermaster (Oceans 8 Films, 2023).
4. Lipscomb, *One Dam at a Time*.
5. John Waldman, conversation with author, May 1, 2023.
6. George Jackman, "The Grandeur of the Hudson's Broad Bays," August 14, 2024. https://www.riverkeeper.org/news-and-events/news-and-updates/the-grandeur-of-the-hudsons-broad-bays.
7. Sarah Mount, email to the author, November 5, 2024.
8. Gretchen Stevens, "Headwater Streams: Values and Threats," webinar, November 3, 2021, https://www.hudsonia.org/2021-events/headwaterstreams.
9. Seth H. Lutter, Scott Cuppett, Suresh A. Sethi, and Brian G. Rahm. "Social considerations for the removal of dams and other aquatic barriers," *BioScience* 74, no. 6 (2024): 393–404, https://doi.org/10.1093/biosci/biae037.
10. Scott Cuppett, "Dams & Culverts: Reconnecting Our Waterways," posted July 5, 2022, by NYSDEC, YouTube, https://www.youtube.com/watch?v=eZmvoVE4dAg.
11. Wallace Nicholls, *Blue Mind* (Little, Brown Spark, 2014), 83.
12. Robert M. Thorson, *The Boatman: Henry David Thoreau's River Years* (Harvard University Press, 2017), 42.
13. John McPhee, *Encounters with the Archdruid* (Farrar, Straus and Giroux, 1971), 159.
14. Lee Briccetti, foreword to *The Poetic Species: A Conversation with Edward O. Wilson and Robert Hass*, by Edward O. Wilson and Robert Hass (Bellevue Literary Press, 2014), 23.

15. Mark Doty, *Heaven's Coast: A Memoir* (HarperPerennial, 1996), 25–26.

16. David Rothenberg, *Secret Sounds of Ponds* (Roof Books, 2023), 21.

17. Wilson, *The Poetic Species*, 51.

18. Raymond Mohl, "The Expressway Teardown Movement in American Cities: Rethinking Postwar Highway Policy in the Post-Industrial Era," *Journal of Planning History* 11, no. 1 (2011): 89–103, https://doi.org/10.1177/1538513211426028.

19. Jedediah Britton-Purdy, "The World We've Built," *Dissent Magazine*, July 3, 2018, https://www.dissentmagazine.org/online_articles/world-we-built-sovereign-nature-infrastructure-leviathan/.

20. Patrick Sisson, "Restoring Nature While Building," *New York Times*, March 16, 2022, p. B7.

21. Lipscomb, *One Dam at a Time*.

22. Waldman, conversation with the author.

23. William H. Schlesinger, "From Headwaters to the Sea," *Translational Ecology* (blog) March 18, 2025, https://blogs.nicholas.duke.edu/citizenscientist/from-headwaters-to-the-sea.

24. Brad Plumer, "Small Streams Vital to Big Waterways, Study Finds," *New York Times*, June 28, 2024, p. A13.

25. James G. Workman, "Dams," in *Encyclopedia of Environmental Ethics and Philosophy* (MacMillan Reference Library, 2009), 198.

26. Steven Hawley, *Cracked: The Future of Dams in a Hot, Chaotic World* (Patagonia, 2023), 129.

27. Lopez, "Lessons from the River," 290.

The Impoundment Preserved

1. Quoted in John McPhee, *Encounters with the Archdruid* (Farrar, Straus and Giroux, 1971), 159.

2. Leo Marx, *The Machine in the Garden* (Oxford University Press, 1964), 251.

3. Gaston Bachelard, *Water and Dreams*, trans. Edith R. Farrell (Pegasus Foundation, Dallas Institute of Humanities and Culture, 1983), 50.

4. Bachelard, *Water and Dreams*, 72.

5. Bachelard, *Water and Dreams*, 68.

6. William H. Schlesinger, "The Source of the Yellow River," *Translational Ecology* (blog), February 8, 2021, https://blogs.nicholas.duke.edu/citizenscientist/the-source-of-the-yellow-river/.

7. Seth H. Lutter, Scott Cuppett, Suresh A. Sethi, and Brian G. Rahm. "Social considerations for the removal of dams and other aquatic barriers," *BioScience* 74, no. 6 (2024): 393–404, https://doi.org/10.1093/biosci/biae037.

8. John Waldman, conversation with the author, Queens College, May 1, 2023.

9. Catrin Einhorn, "A Quarter of Freshwater Fish are at Risk of Extinction, a New Assessment Finds," *New York Times*, December 12, 2023, p. A9.

10. Marlee Tucker, Katrin Böhning-Gaese, William F. Fagan, et al., "Moving in the Anthropocene: Global reductions in terrestrial mammalian movements," *Science* 358, no. 6374 (2018): 466–69.

11. Ben Goldfarb, *Crossings: How Road Ecology is Shaping the Future of the Planet* (W. W. Norton, 2023), 47.

12. Lutter et al., 5.

13. Tom Lewis, *The Hudson: A History* (Yale University Press, 2005), 271.

14. "Reconnaissance for Priority Dam Removal Projects in the Hudson Valley to Improve Herring and Eel Passage," presentation by George Jackman, Riverkeeper, hosted by NYSDEC for the Hudson River Estuary Grants Webinar Series, April 11, 2024.

15. Bachelard, *Water and Dreams*, 55.

16. Peter Gleick, *The Three Ages of Water: Prehistoric Past, Imperiled Present, and a Hope for the Future* (Public Affairs, 2023), 238.

17. Lydia DePillis, "Nature Has Value, Could we Invest in It?," *New York Times*, March 11, 2024, p. B1.

18. Camille Desjonquères, Sara Villén-Pérez, Paulo De Marco, Rafael Márquez, Juan F. Beltrán, and Diego Llusia, "Acoustic species distribution models (aSDMs): A framework to forecast shifts in calling behaviour under climate change," *Methods in Ecology and Evolution* 13, no. 10 (2022): 2089–302. https://doi.org/10.1111/2041-210X.13923.

19. David Rothenberg, *Secret Sounds of Ponds* (Roof Books, 2024), 46.

20. Benjamin L. Gottesman, Gottesman, Dante Francomano, Zhao Zhou, et al., "Acoustic monitoring reveals diversity and surprising dynamics in tropical freshwater soundscapes," *Freshwater Biology* 65, no. 1 (2020): 117–32. https://doi.org/10.1111/fwb.13096.

After the Breach

1. John Waldman, *Running Silver: Restoring Atlantic Rivers and Their Great Fish Migrations* (Lyons Press, 2013), 253.

2. Frank Doherty, "The History of the Clove Valley 1697–1740," *Dutchess County Historical Yearbook* 75 (1990): 33.

3. Gretchen Stevens, "Headwater Streams. Values and Threats," webinar, November 3, 2021, https://www.hudsonia.org/2021-events/headwaterstreams.

4. Gretchen Stevens, "Headwater Streams: Values and Threats," November 3, 2021.

5. Alice B. Outwater, *Water: A Natural History* (Basic Books, 1996), 37.

6. Beth Roessler, "Headwater Streams: Values and Threats," webinar, DEC Hudson River Estuary Program and Cornell University, November 3, 2021.

7. "Key Concepts," Minnesota Department of Resources, https://www.dnr.state.mn.us/whaf/key-concepts/.

8. Stuart Findlay, Cary Institute of Ecosystem Studies, Millbrook, New York, conversation with the author, October 15, 2024.

9. John Waldman, conversation with the author, May 1, 2023.

10. James C. Scott, *In Praise of Floods* (Yale University Press, 2025), 29–31.

11. Mihaly Csikszentmihalyi, *Flow: The Psychology of Optimal Experience* (Harper Perennial, 1991), 6.

12. Wallace J. Nichols, *Blue Mind* (Little, Brown Spark, 2014), 93.

13. Laura Wildman, *One Dam at a Time*, directed by Jon Bowermaster (Oceans Eight Films, 2023).

14. Scott Cuppett and Kiera Healy, "Removing Dams to Benefit Ecology, Community, and Owners," *New York State Conservationist*, October/November 2024, 10–13, https://dec.ny.gov/sites/default/files/2024-12/octnov24consmagweb.pdf.

15. "Beaver Ecology and Management," presented by Michael Fargione, Manager of Field Research & Outdoor Programs, The Cary Institute of Ecosystem Studies, webinar, May 11, 2022.

16. Erica Gies, *Water Always Wins: Thriving in an Age of Drought and Deluge* (University of Chicago Press, 2022), 118.

17. Leila Philip, *Beaverland: How One Weird Rodent Made America* (Twelve Books, 2022, 25.

18. Denise Burchstead, Melinda Daniels, Robert Thorson, and Jason Vokoun, "The River Discontinuum: Applying Beaver Modifications to Baseline Conditions for Restoration of Forested Headwaters," *BioScience* 60, no. 11 (2010): 908–22.

19. Stuart Findlay, conversation with the author, October 15, 2024.

20. Philip, *Beaverland*, 174–75.

21. Judith Schwartz, *Water in Plain Sight* (St. Martin's Press, 2016), 101.

22. Philip, *Beaverland*, 178–79.

23. Maddie Feaster and Matt Best, Riverkeeper, in conversation with the author, October 28, 2024.

The Creek Restored

1. Werner Herzog, *Every Man for Himself and God Against All: A Memoir* (Penguin Press, 2023), 246.

2. William McDermott, "The Rural Hamlet in Dutchess County: An Endangered Species," *Dutchess County Historical Society Yearbook* 71 (1986): 1–10.

3. Alice Outwater, *Water: A Natural History* (Basic Books, 1996), 57.

4. Gretchen Stevens, "Headwater Streams: Values and Threats," webinar, November 3, 2021, https://www.hudsonia.org/2021-events/headwaterstreams.

5. Barry Lopez, "Landscape and Narrative," in *Vintage Lopez* (Vintage Books, 2004), 6.

6. Raymond Zhong, "The Earth's Axis is Shifting, and We're the Reason," *New York Times*, June 29, 2023, p. A1.

7. John Waldman, conversation with the author, May 1, 2023.

8. McDermott, "The Rural Hamlet," in the *Dutchess County Historical Society Yearbook*, 1–2.

Beauty Reconsidered

1. "Archaeological Survey: Oscawana Park & Phase IB" and "Archaeological Survey: Maiden Lane Dam Removal Town of Cortlandt Westchester County, New York," prepared by Stony Creek Archaeology Inc., East Chatham, New York, for the Westchester County Department of Public Works and Transportation, October 2021.

2. John Phillips, conversation with the author, September 27, 2023.

3. Laura Wildman, "Dam Removal: When Less is More," PowerPoint presentation.

4. George Jackman, *Habitat Restoration Along the Hudson*, directed by Jon Bowermaster (Oceans 8 Films, 2021).

5. Wildman, "Dam Removal."

6. Bachelard, *Water and Dreams*, 55.

7. Sallie McFague, *Super, Natural Christians* (Fortress Press, 1977) 28.

8. "Reconnaissance for Priority Dam Removal Projects in the Hudson Valley to Improve Herring and Eel Passage," presentation by George Jackman, Riverkeeper, hosted by NYSDEC for the Hudson River Estuary Grants Webinar Series, April 11, 2024.

9. Maude Salinger, communications coordinator for the Hudson River Estuary Program at the New York State Department of Environmental Conservation, email to the author, June 18, 2024.

10. Eve Sampson, "Dam Collapse Devastates Eastern Sudan," *New York Times*, August 28, 2024, p. A8; Soumya Karlamangla, "Dams Gone, Salmon May Have a Fighting Chance," *New York Times*, August 28, 2024, p. A10.

Streams Reconnected

1. Philip Larkin, "Water," in *Collected Poems*, ed. Anthony Thwaite (Farrar, Strauss and Giroux, 1988), 91.

2. Asher Elbein, "Native Species Hit Hard by Weather Extremes," *New York Times*, November 6, 2023, p. A13.

3. Cianconi, Paolo, Batul Hanife, Francesco Grillo, Sophia Betro, Cokorda Bagus Jaya Lesmana, and Luigi Janiri, "Eco-emotions and Psychoterratic Syndromes:

Reshaping Mental Health Assessment Under Climate Change," *Yale Journal of Biology and Medicine* 96.2 (2023): 211–26.

    4. *The Weight of Nature* by Clayton Page Altern (Dutton, 2024) explores the multiple ways in which the warming climate and its manifestations in such events as extreme heat, wildfires, flooding, and toxic waterways are reconfiguring and otherwise disrupting our neural pathways, in the process derailing memory, language, and other sensory systems.

    5. Rebecca Solnit, introduction to *Embrace Fearlessly the Burning World: Essays* by Barry Lopez (Random House, 2022).

    6. https://largelandscapes.org/natureconnect/

    7. Martin Buber, *I And Thou,* translated by Walter Kaufmann (Charles Scribner's Sons, 1970), 58.

    8. Gavin Schmidt and Zeke Hausfather, "We Study Climate Change. We Can't Explain What We're Seeing," *New York Times,* November 13, 2024, p. SR9.

Acknowledgments

I did not know it at the time, but this book began in tracing the waterways for the Natural Resources Inventory of Union Vale, New York. For that I am indebted to Nate Nardi-Cyrus, report coordinator then at the Hudson River Estuary Program and Sean Carroll, Senior GIS/Environmental Educator at Cornell Cooperative Extension, Dutchess County for their help in guiding us through the project. Betsy Maas, Lisa Martel, Jen Rubbo, Pat Cartalemi, Rachel von Wettberg, and Chris Peterson were others in the town whose work and good will contributed to the NRI.

I treasured those outings with compatriots in the watershed who took me to areas they knew well and whose sense of land and water stewardship nourished the work here. Peter Krulewitch took me to the Clove Spring on a drizzly gray June day. Joe Reilly spent a hot summer afternoon walking me up the Wynants Kill to the site of the old waterwheel. Suzette Lopane walked me and talked me through the stillness and the flow of the Jamawissa, and I am hugely grateful to her. Russ Maxwell and his beautiful mapwork have particular value at this moment when GPS is the more conventional tool for wayfinding. Being on the river with Doug Reed is always a joy—and an education about tides, aquatic plants, water quality. David Rothenberg's improvisational concert at the edge of Furnace Pond introduced me to the sonic life beneath the surface of the water on a cool March morning. Jane Smith, Doug Smith, Hilary Kliros, and Dan Walworth were ever gracious in offering site access, memories, impressions, observations, and notes on history, all of these vital. And gratitude always to George Jackman, who cites Shakespeare in speaking for the fish.

I also thank Anne Kreamer, my longtime pre-editor, who manages to shapeshift my ideas before a word has been written; Jan Hartman for her enthusiasm and support as I began to put this book together; and Julie Hart, a generous and responsive reader. William Schlesinger's insights and thorough evaluation of an early draft were invaluable. After years of using Zoom as mandated by Covid-19, I found that when onsite meetings were not possible I preferred to meet face to face. In the spirit of establishing connectivity, others agreed, and I thank them: Stuart Findlay, David Fischer, Jake Gosnell, Susan Ouellette, Brian Scoralick, John Waldman, John Welsh, and Laura Wildman. I am especially grateful to Fran Dunwell for sharing her wealth of information, her suggestions, her recollections and asides, and most of all for her many years of work on the estuary.

Mark Carabetta, Jeremy Dietrich, Geoffrey Goll, Gareth Hougham, Sergei Krasikov, John Phillips, Warren Shaw, and Chris Solomon were generous with their expertise. At Riverkeeper, John Lipscomb, Leah Rae, Lauren Daisley, Matt Best, and Maddie Feaster stepped in with invaluable help and knowledge. And at the New York State Department of Environmental Conservation, my thanks to Scott Cuppett, Kiera Healy, Beth Roessler, Maude Salinger, Caleigh Millette, Tom Niekrewicz, Anna Palmer, and Sarah Mount, who were unfailingly patient with my constant questions, more questions, and even then, need for follow-ups.

At SUNY Press, Richard Carlin had swift and sure appreciation for the possible merit of a book about these waterways, and my great debt of gratitude goes to him and his entire team at the press: to Julia Cosacchi who guided the manuscript through the publication process sometimes as winding as some of these streams; to copy editor Miranda Dubner whose work in ushering in a final draft was in equal parts incisive and inquisitive; to Ryan Morris for the visual elegance she brought to the design; and to Kate Seburyamo, Jenn Bennett, Tanja Eise, and Julie Fifelski for their efforts to bring this book into the world. I am as grateful to Anne Diggory for allowing me to use her painting "Jammed" on the cover of this book. Her "preference for dynamic instability" captures the spirit of these sites, and I was happy to have her remind me that "Water always makes it through no matter how much piles up."

I am indebted as well to Vicar Richard McKeon and the poetry group he led for several years at the Church of the Messiah in Rhinebeck. He and my compatriots in the group have all indirectly helped me think through some of the ideas here. Eric Karpeles walked the pond loop with me time and again for which I am grateful.

As always, my thanks to Brian, Lucian, and Noel, who remind me daily of the meaning and value of connectivity.

Selected Bibliography

Aldern, Clayton Page. *The Weight of Nature: How a Changing Climate Changes our Brains*. Dutton, 2024.
Bachelard, Gaston. *Water and Dreams: An Essay on the Imagination of Matter*. Translated by Edith R. Farrell. Pegasus Foundation, Dallas Institute of Humanities and Culture, 1983.
Blaugrund, Annette, Betti-Sue Hertz, Elizabeth Hutchinson, and Dorothy M. Peteet. *Shifting Shorelines: Art, Industry, and Ecology Along the Hudson River*. Wallach Art Gallery, Columbia University, 2024.
Boyle, Robert H. *The Hudson River: A Natural and Unnatural History*. W. W. Norton & Company, 1969.
Gies, Erica. *Water Always Wins: Thriving in an Age of Drought and Deluge*. University of Chicago Press, 2022.
Gleick, Peter. *The Three Ages of Water: Prehistoric Past, Imperiled Present, and a Hope for the Future*. Public Affairs, 2023.
Goldfarb, Ben. *Crossings: How Road Ecology is Shaping the Future of the Planet*. W. W. Norton & Company, 2023.
Grossman, Elizabeth. *Watershed: The Undamming of America*. Counterpoint Press, 2002.
Hawley, Steven. *Cracked: The Future of Dams in a Hot, Chaotic World*. Patagonia, 2023.
Leopold, Luna, M. Gordon Wolman, and John P. Miller. *Fluvial Processes in Geomorphology*. W. H. Freeman and Company, 1964.
Lewis, Tom. *The Hudson: A History*. Yale University Press, 2005.
Lopez, Barry. *Embrace Fearlessly the Burning World: Essays*. Random House, 2022.
Lopez, Barry. *Vintage Lopez*. Vintage Books, 2004.
Marx, Leo. *The Machine in the Garden: Technology and the Pastoral Ideal in America*. Oxford University Press, 1964
McFague, Sallie. *Super Natural Christians: How We Should Love Nature*. Fortress Press, 1997.

Macfarlane, Robert. *Is a River Alive?* W. W. Norton & Company, 2025.
McPhee, John. *Encounters with the Archdruid.* Farrar, Straus and Giroux, 1971.
Nash, Roderick Frazier. *Wilderness and the American Mind.* 5th ed. Yale University Press, 2014.
Nichols, Wallace J. *Blue Mind: The Surprising Science That Shows How Being Near, In, On, or Under Water Can Make You Happier, Healthier, More Connected and Better at What You Do.* Little, Brown Spark, 2014.
Outwater, Alice B. *Water: A Natural History.* Basic Books, 1996.
Philip, Leila. *Beaverland: How One Weird Rodent Made America.* Twelve Books, 2022.
Rothenberg, David. *Secret Sounds of Ponds.* Roof Books, 2023.
Sante, Lucy. *Nineteen Reservoirs: On their Creation and the Promise of Water for New York City.* The Experiment, 2022.
Schwartz, Judith. *Water in Plain Sight.* St. Martin's Press, 2016.
Scott, James C. *In Praise of Floods: The Untamed River and the Life It Brings.* Yale University Press, 2025.
Thorson, Robert M. *The Boatman: Henry David Thoreau's River Years.* Harvard University Press, 2017.
Waldman, John. *Runing Silver: Restoring Atlantic Rivers and Their Great Fish Migrations.* Lyons Press, 2013.
Wilson, Edward O., and Robert Hass. *The Poetic Species: A Conversation with Edward O. Wilson and Robert Hass.* Bellevue Literary Press, 2014.
Wilson, Edward O. *Biophilia: The Human Bond with Other Species.* Harvard University Press, 1984.

Index

9/11 Memorial, 32

Abbey, Edward, 16, 42
Adirondack mountains, 6
Aitchison, Dan, 126
ailanthus, 79
Albany (NY), 47
alder. *See under* trees
alewife. *See* herring
algae blooms, 12, 35–36, 49, 51, 137, 143
American Fisheries Society, 73, 138. *See also* fisheries
American Rivers, 7, 24
anadromous fish, 9; bass, 7, 9, 45, 65, 126–127; herring: 3, 5, 7, 9, 23, 104, 115, 117, 131, 147; shad (American), 7, 19; sturgeon, 9, 142
Arad, Michael, 32
Arba'at Dam, 130
Army Corps of Engineers, 116, 145
Arnold, David, 85–86
ash. *See under* trees
Ashbery, John, 148

Bachelard, Gaston, 31–32, 35, 49, 60, 120
barberry, 39, 59, 63, 79, 122

bass. *See under* anadromous fish
bats, 129, 137
Beacon (NY), 141, 144
bears, 78, 105, 127
beavers, 62–63, 68–69, 70, 76, 78, 94, 114
beech. *See under* trees
Beech Leaf Disease, 121
Beekman (NY), 25
Best, Matthew, 83
Biden, Joseph R. Jr., 20
Billerica (MA), 19
bioacoustics, 53–55, 138
biodiversity, 7–8, 22–23, 38, 40, 115, 132
Biohabitats (engineering firm), 146
Bipartisan Infrastructure Law, 139
birch. *See under* trees
birds: duck, 62, 76, 120; eagle (bald), 9, 62, 70–71, 116, 129, 142; egrets, 46, 49; heron (blue), 62–63, 69, 94, 104; migration, 80, 120; swan, 62
bittersweet, 39, 63
bluegill. *See* resident fish
Blue Mind. *See* Nichols, Wallace
Bolivia, 39
borrow pits, 112
breaching. *See under* dams

bridges, 1–2, 27, 48, 79–80, 85, 117, 139
Brower, David, 29
Brown, Tracy, 44. See also Riverkeeper
brownfield sites. See under industry
Buber, Martin, 140, 149
bullheads. See under resident fish
Burden Ironworks, 2
Burden Pond, 2, 5

caddisflies. See under insects
cadmium, 43–44
Carson, Rachel, 17, 128, 139
catadromous fish, 9; eel (American), 4–5, 7–10, 76, 87, 92, 104–105, 115, 117, 120, 124–127, 131, 138, 147, 149
catfish. See under potadromous fish
cattails, 2, 63, 71, 83
charismatic megafauna, 127
Charles River, 24
chestnut (American). See under trees
chlorophyll, 121
City University of New York, 38–39
climate change, 6–7, 12, 24, 35, 53, 80, 103, 113, 120–121, 137, 143; and biodiversity loss, 40, 143, 147, 156n4
Clove Mountain, 59
Clove Spring, 59
Con Edison, 131–132
Concord River, 19
concrete: as barrier, 5, 70, 87–88, 144; Cyclopean, 87; degraded, 30, 41, 60, 86, 90; removal, 21, 25, 90–91, 110, 117, 146–148; as stabilization, 43. See also dams: spillways
Connecticut River, 71–72
connectivity: as concept, 16, 18, 82, 93, 96–97, 106–107, 138–140; hyper-, 148–149; of waterways, 8–9, 23, 38, 61, 72–73, 79, 117, 138. See also streams
construction (general), 20, 27, 39, 73–74, 91, 94, 105, 118. See also dams: construction
contamination. See industry: pollution and debris and sediment: contamination
continuum (as concept), 64–65, 69–70, 87, 103, 140
Cornell University: Cooperative Extension, xi; Department of Natural Resources, 92; K. Lisa Yang Center for Conservation Bioacoustics, 54; Water Resources Institute, 3, 12, 90, 93
Cortlandt (NY), 12, 27, 110, 116, 146
cottonwood. See under trees
Coulter, Ryan, 93
crabs: blue, 117; mitten, 124
crappie. See under potadromous fish
crayfish, 100–101, 125–126
Creighton, James, 146
Crouse's Store, 58
culture, 12, 18, 41–42, 112, 115, 135, 144
Cuppett, Scott, 12–13, 63, 66, 81, 92, 129, 146
current. See water: lentic/lotic systems

dace. See under potadromous fish
damage. See under dams: impacts on environment
dams: breaching, 11, 13, 16, 25, 36, 44–46, 51, 56–59, 61, 79, 82, 90, 130; as concept, 15–16; construction, 2, 7, 11–12, 24, 27, 30, 42–43, 52, 57, 67, 87, 146; design, 50, 87; first barrier, 3, 5, 12, 37, 105, 110, 117, 144–145;

functionality, 7–8, 10–11, 13, 22, 24, 27, 34, 52, 67, 80, 101, 110, 145; as hazards, 12, 37, 40, 47, 51, 68, 78–79, 87–90, 129, 144; gates (flood or sluice), 3, 6, 10, 90; impacts on environment, 7, 9, 19, 23, 40, 42, 74, 87, 92, 132, 144; inventoried status, xii, 6–7, 24, 40; neglect, 50, 57, 67; removal, xii, 3–12, 15–16, 21, 24–25, 36–38, 40–41, 43–44, 51–52, 61, 73, 85–92, 110, 114, 117–119, 129–132, 144–147; removal costs/challenges, 37, 67–68, 88–90, 93, 116–117, 120–121, 123, 129; restoration, 47, 131; spillways, 3–4, 13, 16, 36, 43, 47–49, 51, 58, 68, 117; stability, 36, 40, 42–43, 47, 51.
damselflies. *See under* insects
danger. *See* dams: as hazards
Darwin, Charles, 17–18
deconstruction. *See also* dams: removal
deer, 11, 61–62, 77–78, 105, 112, 122
DeLucia, David, 116
Department of Natural Resources. *See under* Cornell University
Desjonquères, Camille, 53
development. *See* construction (general)
diadromous fish, 8, 37–38. *See also* anadromous fish *and* catadromous fish
Dietrich, Jeremy, 92
diseases, 50, 81, 112, 121–122, 137
disturbance ecology, 22
Division of Water, Bureau of Flood Protection and Dam Safety. *See under* New York State Department of Environmental Conservation
Doty, Mark, 18

dragonflies. *See under* insects
dredging, 37, 44, 112–113, 115, 132
drought, 30, 49, 51, 60, 77, 103, 146
ducks. *See under* birds
duckweed, 132
Dunwell, Frances, 8–10, 51, 105, 127, 138, 143
Dutchess County: Historical Society, 107; Natural Resources Inventory, 142–143; Soil and Water Conservation District, 89–90

eagles (bald). *See under* birds
ecological succession, 75, 78, 83
economics, 9–10, 20, 24, 42, 52, 67, 86, 148
Ecuador, 39
educational efforts, 4, 9–10, 116, 121, 124–126, 138, 142
eel (American). *See under* catadromous fish
egrets. *See under* birds
electrofishing, 104, 124–126
Elwha River, 24
emerald ash borer. *See under* insects
End of Nature, The. See McKibben, Bill
endangered species, 10, 69, 141
engineering, 72–73
Environmental Protection Agency (EPA), 44
eremocene, 137, 140
erosion, 46, 65, 69, 101, 145; control, 4, 61–62, 76, 92, 96, 121
estuaries, 8–9, 27, 115, 127, 138
eutrophication, 49, 120

factories. *See under* industry
fallfish. *See under* potadromous fish
farming. *See under* industry
Feinberg, Lindsey, 121–123
ferns, 31, 75, 98, 110, 122–123

Findlay, Stuart, 70
fireweed, 76
Fish and Wildlife Service Program, 3
fish: economic importance, 9–10; habitats, 3–5, 7–9, 35, 44; migration, 3–10, 12, 19–20, 23–24, 37–38, 40–41, 61, 68, 73, 77, 87, 90, 93, 104–105, 120, 124, 131, 144–145; spawning, 3–4, 6, 9, 60, 95, 124, 131; stocking, 46. *See also* anadromous, catadromous, *and* potadromous fish
fisheries, 9–10, 65, 73
fishing, 2, 8, 10, 32, 40, 65, 109, 141–142
Fishkill Creek, 10, 27, 30, 36–37, 46, 59–60, 141, 144, 149
Fishkill Creek Watershed Alliance, 142
Fitzgerald, F. Scott. 42
flood: control, 4, 7–8, 12–13, 19, 24, 34, 42, 52, 60–61, 68; frequency, 7, 11, 40, 49–50, 76, 145
floodplains, 8, 11, 13, 22, 41, 48, 61–64, 66, 68, 73–78, 81–83, 118, 122, 142–143; as stabilization, 62
flow. *See* water: lentic/lotic systems
forests: clearing/cutting, 29, 78, 92, 105, 111, 113, 115, 123; creation, 11, 58, 62, 71, 74–76, 81–83, 133; disease/stress, 50, 81, 111–112, 121; preserving, 52; symbolism, 112
Fort Edwards (NY), 44
foxes, 78
frogs, 69
Frost, Robert, 31
Furnace Creek. *See* Jamawissa Creek
Furnace Brook. *See* Jamawissa Creek
Furnace Pond, 10, 16, 20, 27–30, 33–57, 61, 115, 149

garlic mustard, 110, 122–123

gates. *See under* dams
General Electric, 44, 131
ghost dams. *See* dams: inventoried status
ghost waters. *See* streams: ephemerality
Goll, Geoffrey, 118, 131, 133, 138
Gosnell, Jake, 45–46, 51
Gottesman, Benjamin, 54
Grand Teton Mountains, 32
grants, 8, 10, 37, 89, 93, 132, 143–144. *See also* dams: removal costs
grasses: broadleaf box, 123; fowl manna, 121; native, 11, 56, 59–60, 121, 123; stabilizing, 46, 78, 92, 121; stiltgrass, 71, 83. *See also* sedges
grape (wild), 74
groundhogs, 62, 99
Guide to the Lakes. *See* Wordsworth, William
Gulf of Mexico, 36

Hass, Robert: "On Rivers & Stories," 16–17
headwater streams, 12, 60–61, 64–65, 105, 140
hemlock. *See under* trees
hemlock wooly adelgid. *See under* insects
heron (blue). *See under* birds
herring. *See under* anadromous fish
Herzog, Werner, 85
Hibernian (NY), 25, 85, 107
hickory. *See under* trees
Hilltop Hanover Farm, 121
Hoagland, Tony, 17, 77–78
Hochul, Kathy, 80
Hogansburg Dam, 144
Holden Dam, 145
honeysuckle, 79, 122
Hougham, Gareth, 145–147

Hudson, Henry, 109
Hudson Basin River Watch, 4
Hudson Falls (NY), 44
Hudson River, 1–10, 12, 22–23, 37, 98, 108–109, 115–116, 131, 135–136, 143–145, 149; watershed, 3, 5–7, 70, 144
Hudson River Estuary Program (NYSDEC), 3–4, 8–10, 12, 37, 61, 81, 89, 93, 97–98, 127, 143, 146
Hudson River School, 135
Hudson River Sloop Clearwater, 146
Hudson Valley Stream Conservancy, 145
hurricanes, 47–48, 76, 78, 80, 87, 90, 95, 137
hydrological signals, 23, 38. *See also* fish: migration
hydropower, 2, 6–7, 24, 34, 48, 52, 58, 67, 86, 130, 143–144. *See also* dams

I and Thou. *See* Buber, Martin
impoundments, 27, 29, 43
Indian Point Energy Center, 116
industry: brickmaking, 110, 112; factories, 1–2, 4, 144; farming, 19, 22, 29, 40, 49, 107; general, 2–3, 6–7, 10–11, 20, 30, 41, 144; mills, xi, 2, 27, 57–58, 85–86, 88, 106; mining/smelting, 2, 13, 29–30, 39, 41, 44, 52, 58, 67, 144; pollution and debris, 2–5, 10–12, 20, 22, 35–37, 40–41, 43–45, 49, 73, 112, 128; railroads, 2, 86, 109–110, 114–116, 131, 141
Inflation Reduction Act (2022), 20
Infrastructure, 20, 39, 114, 117, 139. *See also* Bipartisan Infrastructure Law
insects, 4, 52, 69, 100–101; cabbage moth, 99, 125, caddisfly, 92, 100–101; damselfly, 100–101; dragonfly, 100–101; emerald ash borer, 49–50, 111; hemlock wooly adelgid, 39, 50; spongy moth, 52, 80–81; stonefly, 92, 100; water boatman, 54; water penny, 100–101
International Union for Conservation of Nature, 39–40
invasive species, 40, 62–63, 71, 74, 80, 122, 125–126. *See also* insects *and* nonnative species

Jackman, George, 7, 26, 38–42, 48–49, 74–75, 77, 83, 116–117, 128, 131, 140, 146–147. *See also* Riverkeeper
Jamawissa Creek, 12, 27, 108–133, 149; meaning, 114
Japanese knotweed. *See* knotweeds
Jenny Lake, 32
jewelweed, 39, 71, 76, 83, 125
Johnstown (PA), 13
jumpseed, 122
Jung, Carl, 106, 112

Keats, Jonathon, 103
Klamath River, 130
Klamath River Renewal Corporation, 24
Kliros, Hilary 86, 88–91, 93–97, 102, 106
knotweeds (*polygonum sp.*), 1, 49, 59, 71, 76, 83, 122. *See also* jumpseed

lakes, 11, 14, 23, 26, 31–34, 39, 77, 132, 143, 145–146; glacial, 32, 71, 74
"Landscape and Narrative." *See* Lopez, Barry
landscaping. *See* restorative landscaping. *See also* planting (of saplings and seedlings)

Index | 165

Larkin, Philip, 135
legislation/-ors, 39, 42, 75, 121
Lenni Lenape, 27. *See also* Native Americans
Lennon, John, 119
lentic water. *See* water: lentic/lotic systems
Leopold, Luna, 46
Lincoln Memorial, 32, 36
Literature of Place, A. See Lopez, Barry
Lipscomb, John, 3–5, 23. *See also* Riverkeeper
locust (black). *See under* trees
Long Island (NY), 38–39
loosestrife, 59, 71, 74, 83, 125
Lopane, Suzette, 111–116, 118, 120–123, 127–130, 132, 146
Lopez, Barry, 1, 138; "Landscape and Narrative," 97; *A Literature of Place*, 25; "The Naturalist," 82
lotic water. *See* water: lentic/lotic systems

Maine, 24
maple. *See under* trees
maps, 14, 35, 57, 59, 105, 112–114, 141–144
marshes. *See* wetlands
Marx, Leo, 30
Massachusetts, 24
Maxwell, Russell, 141
McAndrews estate, 110–111, 116
McFague, Sally, 122–123, 140
McKibben, Bill [William], 19
McKinney, Glenn Ford, 58
McKinney Dam, 11, 27, 45, 57–83; breach, 57–58, 61, 70, 76, 79, 82; construction of, 57; floodplain, 74
McKinney Pond, 56, 58, 61, 65, 82
McPhee, John, 17
meadowing, 11, 59–63, 76, 78, 97, 119

Millette, Caleigh, 98–102, 124, 126
mills. *See under* industry
mink, 76, 86–87, 95
Mount, Sarah, 124–127
mudflats, 2, 11, 57–59, 69
mugwort, 97, 125
multiflora, 39, 110
music. *See* bioacoustics
muskrats, 76

National Fish and Wildlife Foundation, 144; grants, 144
National Parks Service: RAD framework, 130
Native Americans, 39, 41, 109, 115, 144, 148
native species, 21, 24, 43, 39, 60–63, 71, 76–77, 82–83, 112–114, 121–123, 137, 144. *See also* nonnative species
"Naturalist, The." *See* Lopez, Barry
Natural Resources Inventory, xi
Naugatuck River (CT), 73
nettles, 71, 74
Newburgh (NY), 145
New York City, 6, 20
New York Harbor, 8
New York State Department of Environmental Conservation (NYSDEC), xi, 11, 16, 25, 77, 79, 89–91, 93, 120, 124, 129; Division of Water, Bureau of Flood Protection and Dam Safety, 47, 88, 129; funding/grants, 3–4, 132; permits, 116, 120–121, 123, 128–133, 145; regulations, 37, 42–43, 47, 107, 112, 131–132. *See also* Hudson River Estuary Program *and* Trees for Tribs
New York State Water Resources Institute. *See under* Cornell University

New Zealand, 39
Nichols, Wallace, 14
Niekrewicz, Thomas, 98–101, 105
nitrogen, 36, 49
nonnative species, 4, 7, 39, 63, 73, 111–114, 122, 124, 136. *See also* invasive species *and* insects
Norquist, John, 20
nostalgia, 20, 41–42
NYSDEC. *See* New York State Department of Environmental Conservation

oak. *See under* trees
Odum, Eugene, 75
Oliver, Mary, 122
"On Rivers & Stories." *See* Hass, Robert
Oscawana Park and Nature Preserve, 27, 110, 121
otters, 117
ownership (of property), 10, 16, 22–23, 65, 68, 79, 88–89, 110, 144
oysters, 115

parks, 2, 12, 30, 50, 133
Passive Acoustic Monitoring, 54. *See also* bioacoustics
pathing, 104–105, 112
Pennsylvania, 13, 24, 128
Penobscot River, 24
perch. *See under* potadromous fish
permits, 25, 88–89, 91, 98, 100, 116, 120–121, 123, 127–133, 145
Phillips, John, 115–117
phragmites, 2, 63, 109
phosphorus, 36, 49
pike. *See under* potadromous fish
pine (white). *See under* trees
planting (of saplings/seedlings), 21, 58, 61–64, 73–76, 82–83, 89, 92, 96, 113–114, 117, 121–123, 139;

polyvinyl tubing, 11, 62, 64, 74, 77, 81, 83
poetry, 17–18, 31, 77, 135, 148
poison ivy, 123
politics, 37, 42, 46, 51, 72–73, 75
pollution. *See under* industry
polychlorinated biphenyls (PCBs), 44
polycyclic aromatic hydrocarbons (PAHs), 45, 128
polyvinyl tubing. *See under* planting
ponds, 14–15, 18, 26, 30, 33; as concept, 15, 26, 31–33 *See also* Furnace Pond
pools: as concept, 31–32, 49, 67; manmade, 60; vernal, 14
porcelain berry, 39, 125
possums, 45, 94
potadromous fish: catfish, 45, 76, 126; crappie, 76; dace, 93, 126; fallfish, 126; perch, 4, 76; pike, 76; sucker, 4, 7, 93, 117, 124, 126–127; trout, 24, 30, 46, 60, 65, 46, 74, 76, 93, 117, 142, 144
Powell, John Wesley, 15
Pray Pond, 37, 59, 141
Princeton Hydro, 118. *See also* Goll, Geoffrey

Quassaick Creek, 145

Railroad Pond, 131
railroads. *See under* industry
rainfall, 6–7, 12–13, 48, 51, 78–80, 87, 103, 118–119, 130, 145–146. *See also* hurricanes
removal. *See under* dams
recreation, 2–3, 8, 10–12, 24, 34, 37, 46, 50, 132, 145
Reed, Doug, 4
reservoirs, 7, 22–23, 34, 67
resident fish: bluegill, 93; bullhead, 93; sunfish, 76, 93, 124, 126–127

restorative landscaping: 4, 11–13, 19–22, 25, 36–37, 43, 91–93, 104, 113–114, 117, 119. *See also* planting (of saplings and seedlings)
rivers, 8, 14–17, 19, 103; continuum concept, 64–65, 69–70, 87; –time, 103–104 *See also* Hudson River, streams
riverbank. *See* shoreline
Riverkeeper, 3, 7, 26, 39, 44, 61, 81, 83, 129, 144, 146. *See also* Trout Unlimited
road ecology, 20, 105, 118, 139
Roessler, Beth, 81–82
Rothenberg, David, 18, 53–55, 138
Roundhouse Dam, 144
Rousseau, Jean-Jacques, 14
rushes, 62, 74

safety (public). *See* dams: as hazards
Saint Regis Mohawk Tribe, 144
Saint Regis River, 144
salmon, 24, 131, 144
Sargasso Sea, 9, 124
Scoralick, Brian, 79–80
Sea Around Us, The. See Carson, Rachel
Secret Sounds of Ponds. See Rothenburg, David
sedges, 11, 26, 61–62, 74, 76; *Carex sp.*, 123; sawgrass, 11, 59
sediment: accumulation, 2–3, 12, 23–24, 30, 34, 38, 40, 44, 46, 48–49, 58, 61; contamination, 43–45, 128, 131–132; deficit, 111; flow, 2–5, 7, 23, 30, 32, 40, 44–46, 61, 92, 118, 128; stability/removal, 11, 25, 37, 44, 46, 62
shad. *See under* anadromous fish
Shapp Pond (and dam), 11, 27, 84–107
Shaw, Warren, 47
shoreline: ecology, 4, 41, 46, 64; stabilization, 4, 21, 46, 89, 92–93

silt. *See* sediment
skunk cabbage, 75, 112
slag. *See* industry: mining/smelting
snakes, 76
Solnit, Rebecca, 138
sounds (of water), 18, 36
spicebush, 123
spillways. *See under* dams
spongy moths. *See under* insects
springs, 60
Sprout Brook/Creek, 134, 145–147
Sprout Lake, 145–146
spruce (Norway). *See under* trees
stagnation. *See under* water
Stanne, Stephen, 146
stewardship (of land), 17–20, 22–23, 47, 50, 122
still (water). *See* water: lentic/lotic systems
stiltgrass. *See under* grasses
stoneflies. *See under* insects
stream: bends/meanders, 64–66, 81, 94; ephemerality, 23, 48, 64; fragmentation, 7, 65, 69, 147
sturgeon. *See under* anadromous fish
sublime (in landscape), 135–136
sucker (white). *See under* potadromous fish
sunfish. *See under* resident fish
swans. *See under* birds
sycamore. *See under* trees

Taj Mahal, 32
Taylor, Ryan, 147
tearthumb, 76
thalweg, 79
Thoreau, Henry David, 14–15, 19, 30; *Walden*, 31, 33; *A Week on the Concord and Merrimack Rivers*, 19
Thorson, Robert M., 15
tides, 8, 21, 109, 111, 115, 145; and aquatic life, 6, 9, 115, 143
Tierney, Jim, 120

time (as concept), 103. *See also* continuum
Tioronda Dam, 144
Tioronda Hat Works, 144
transitional areas, 4, 8, 53, 83
transpiration, 77–78
trash (non-industrial), 2–3, 35, 87–88, 90, 97
trees: alder, 82; ash, 30, 49–50, 52, 111; beech, 83, 111, 121–122; birch, 11, 61, 78, 83, 111; chestnut (American), 52; cottonwood, 61, 63, 82; dogwood, 61, 77, 83, 92, 111; gum, 83; hemlock, 30, 50, 52; hickory, 30, 60, 110; ironwood, 83, 110; locust (black), 111, 113; maple, 11, 30, 60–61, 77–78, 82–83, 110–113; oak, 30, 32, 52, 60, 74, 77–78, 81–83, 110–112, 122; pine, 11, 30, 58, 61, 83; spruce (Norway), 58; for shade, 62; sycamore, 11, 61, 77, 82–83; tulip, 111–113, 122; willow, 2, 6, 59, 61, 74, 77, 81–83. *See also* forests
Trees for Tribs, 61, 74, 81, 92
tributaries, 1, 4–9, 22–25, 27, 83, 90, 95, 110, 124, 138, 140, 143, 148–149; as concept, 63, 67, 83
Troy (New York), 1–4, 8
trout. *See under* potadromous fish
Trout Unlimited, 81. *See also* Riverkeeper
toxins. *See under* industry
tulip trees. *See under* trees
turbidity. *See* water: quality *and* sediment
turtles, 69, 94, 125, 141

Union Vale, 37
United Arab Emirates, 40
United Nations, 40
United States Army Corps of Engineers, 116, 145
United States Department of the Interior, 143–144
United States Environmental Protection Agency (EPA), 44
United States Fish and Wildlife Service Program, 3
United States Forest Service, 48

verbena, 61–62, 76
vernal pools. *See under* pools
vervain. *See* verbena

Walden. *See* Thoreau, Henry David
Walden Pond. *See* Thoreau, Henry David
Waldman, John, 37–39, 57, 61, 65, 104, 146
Wappinger Creek, 27, 85, 90, 93, 97–100, 105, 148
Washington (state), 24
Washington Monument, 32
water: lentic/lotic systems, 13–16, 22, 35, 48, 64, 67, 70, 92, 96, 109, 140; quality, 4–5, 7–8, 12, 15, 23, 35, 37, 49, 61, 73, 90, 92, 98–100, 104, 129, 144–145; stagnation, 33–35, 49, 51, 117
water boatman. *See under* insects
water penny. *See under* insects
waterfalls: natural, 2, 5, 9, 69, 95, 135; artificial, 9, 15–16, 36, 86, 96, 144
Webster, Jean, 58
Week on the Concord and Merrimack Rivers, A. *See* Thoreau, Henry David
Weill, Simone, 123
Welsh, John, 46–47
Westchester County (NY), 110–111, 116, 121, 145–146
wetlands, 3, 8, 43, 68–69, 76, 112, 145; endangered, 24, 52, 115, 132, 143; species in, 59, 62, 69, 74, 77, 112, 121

Wildman, Laura, 71–73, 109, 113–114, 117, 119, 138–139, 146
willow. *See under* trees
Wilson, Edward Osborne, 17–18, 42, 137
Wilson, Joshua, 146
wineberry, 123
witch hazel, 121
wooly adelgid. *See* insects: hemlock wooly adelgid
Wordsworth, William: *Guide to the Lakes*, 34
Wynants Kill, 1–6, 10, 27
Wyoming, 32

www.ingramcontent.com/pod-product-compliance
Lightning Source LLC
Chambersburg PA
CBHW021157160426
43194CB00007B/773